Tucks Textures
& Pleats

Jennie Rayment

Acknowledgements

This book is dedicated to all my friends, family and my husband Nick - without their mutual support and help, none of the amazing things that have since occurred would ever have happened.

My heartfelt thanks are extended especially to Basil Crisp (sadly no longer with us) and Nick Diment for their unflagging help in proof reading and correcting all the horrendous mistakes. Geoff Mullery for his kindness in converting the original Word Processor discs to a usable format; Shelagh Jarvis for all her help in making samples and the beautiful quilt in addition to her friendship and support over many years; Sue Wood, Anne Smith, Lesley Seddon and Chris Frampton for the loan of their work for the photographs; Margot Abrahams and Angie McKimm for their splendid ideas and Elizabeth Cobbett for the loan of her photocopier (sadly now defunct).

Also a thank you to John Plimmer, the photographer and Derry Morgan, the printer without whose initial help and advice this book would not have been such a best seller over the years.

Finally, I thank all the students who have suffered my teaching and returned for more! Without the inspiration of teaching and meeting so many delightful people, my life would have been very empty.

Copyright © Jennie Rayment 2012
First published November 1994
Revised and reprinted 1996/1997/1998/2000/2003/2005/2008
Revised, reprinted & extended 2012/2014

J. R. Publications
5 Queen Street, Emsworth,
Hampshire, PO10 7BJ. England UK
Tel/Fax: +44 (0)1243 374860
e-mail: jenrayment@aol.com
web site: www.jennierayment.com

Printed by Holbrooks Printers Ltd
Norway Road, Hilsea
Portsmouth, Hampshire PO3 5HX. England
Tel: 02392 661485 Fax: 02392 671119
e-mail: mail@holbrooks.com

ISBN - 13: 978-0-95-24675-8-8
ISBN - 10: 0-9524675-8-5

Tiles and Pottery kindly loaned by Zydeco. Tel: 01705 469119

Contents

Introduction

Tantalise with Tucks.
Beguile with the Bias.
Enter the fascinating world of textural creativity!

Be guided through the tactile delights of fabric manipulation. Discover the simplicity of the techniques and explore the diversity, as you create a unique masterpiece.

It's easy, it's fun and it's different,
and making mistakes will not matter!

I have been teaching these methods for a number of years, and there is nothing nicer than being able to reassure new students...

"Every one can make all these exciting and innovative textural creations. The ability to sew a straight line is not really necessary - it's helpful, but the end product may be better, certainly different, with a few added minor deviations. After all, variety is the spice of life!"

Very little equipment is required. The samples can be stitched by hand or machine - a basic sewing machine will cope with all these techniques. An accurate seam allowance is not always essential, the designs can be planned as you sew, changes can be made and only you will know if the final result is perhaps not quite your original intention!

Now a word of warning for all those from the USA who read this book - in the UK calico is an unbleached cotton cloth not a floral printed cotton fabric! Do not be puzzled - I had no clue when I first wrote this book that unbleached cotton cloth wasn't called calico in every country. I have learnt since.

`Experience is the name everyone gives to their mistakes' (Oscar Wilde 1892)

****

Have confidence in your abilities, read the text and try a little textured twiddling!

So... Gather up the fabric, collect your equipment,
clear a space on the table, frozen t.v. dinner tonight, and let's begin!

Equipment and Fabrics

The basic essentials that most students will find most useful (in addition to the usual sewing accessories) are:

1. Rotary cutter
2. Ruler for use with rotary cutter
3. Cutting mat
4. Hand or electric sewing machine.

A sewing machine is not necessary as all the techniques may be done by hand, but it does speed up the process.

Rotary Cutters

There are many different cutters to choose from these days in a variety of sizes. The 45mm sized blade is probably the most popular choice as opposed to the smaller 28mm size or the larger 60mm one. If you have any difficulty in grasping tools select a cutter with an ergonomic handle as this may be more comfortable to hold.

When buying a rotary cutter for the first time, remember to slacken the screw on the back of the cutter before beginning any cutting to allow the blade to rotate completely. (This information is not always included in instructions.) After you have used the cutter several times, the screw can loosen and the blade will rotate properly. At this point you may find that the blade will only partially cut the fabric, due to the over-use of one section of the wheel.

Once you have finished cutting, tighten the screw again to prevent the guard sliding back when the cutter is not in use.

**DO NOT TO FORGET TO REPLACE THE GUARD
IMMEDIATELY YOU HAVE MADE ANY CUT.**

Too many accidents are caused by open blades.

There are some makes of cutters that have an automatically retracting guard - it retracts as soon as pressure is applied. This might be a more useful gadget to purchase for arthritic or less flexible hands. Be careful when this type of cutter is accidentally pushed across any surface other than a recommended cutting mat as it will make a mark. Not only will an unguarded cutter blade scratch the surface of that prized piece of furniture but the blade will blunt very rapidly.

Using the Cutter

Some people have difficulty cutting with this tool. A few problems that occur are:

1. Failure to cut the beginning/end of the fabric.

Start the cutting slightly before the beginning of the material and run the cutter off the end of the cloth.

2. Failure to cut through all the layers.

Apply firmer pressure to the cutter as you cut, the blade will not damage the board. Push the cutter away from you. In my opinion, it is not a good idea to pull the blade towards the body and if you slip, then you may easily cut yourself. Stay safe and push the blade away from your body.

3. Failure to cut straight lines.

Ensure the blade is next to the ruler, the guard on the cutter is on the outside away from the ruler. Iron the fabric before cutting. Check that the material is folded flat with no creases.

<u>Rotary Cutting Mats</u>

There are many different mats on the market. Some are 'self-healing' so the surface cannot be damaged with cutting, providing the blade is intact. Try not to 'saw' through any uncut portion of fabric as small slivers of the mat could be removed from the surface of the board. The non-self-healing mats will damage with use, but are less expensive.

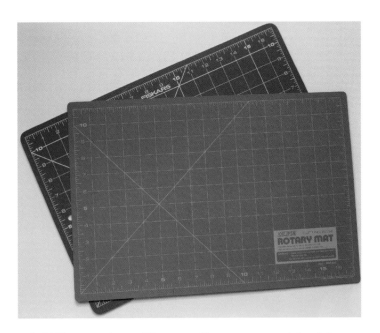

When purchasing a mat, there are several different sizes. The smaller ones are ideal for carrying to classes, but the available surface area is not so useful for cutting large strips. The medium size 17″ x 23″ (43cm x 60cm) is a good size for most projects.

Some mats have grid and angle lines superimposed; these are helpful for lining up the material, but not totally necessary if you possess a Rotary Cutting Ruler (see below). Whichever mat you finally select, keep it flat at all times, and please do not leave it in the sun as the excessive heat will warp the surface. It appears that nothing will remove those wrinkles and you can't give it a face lift!

Rotary Cutting Rulers

Once again, as there is a tremendous choice and variety on the market, you can quickly be bamboozled into purchasing more rulers than you need. I would recommend starting with the large 6/6½" x 24" (15/16cm x 60cm). Most cutting tasks can be performed with this sized ruler. The only drawback may be the overall length and you may prefer a smaller one if working space is tight. As with all things, everyone has a personal preference, and what is suitable for you may not be someone else's choice. Check that the selected rotary cutting ruler measures accurately. As the printed lines are often fairly thick, it is important to discover which part of the line relates to the accurate measurement. Test the spacing of the lines with another ruler - metal ones often give the most accurate measurements. For the most of the designs in this book, there is no need for absolute accuracy; often a straight cut is all that is required.

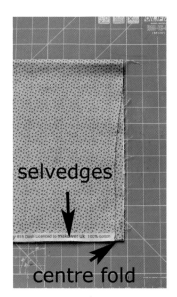

selvedges

centre fold

Measuring with the Rotary Cutting Ruler

Confusion can strike when you are first faced with all these new gadgets. All you wish to do is to cut a strip off the cloth. Easy really! Right-handed people try this method - for those who are left-handed reverse the directions (looking at the pictures in a mirror helps).

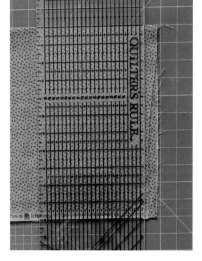

1. Press the fabric first. Fold in half lining up the selvedges, re-fold again, matching the centre fold to the selvedges.

cut

2. Before cutting any width, trim the beginning of the cloth (it may be unevenly cut).

Place the ruler completely on top of the fabric; check that the folds are parallel with the lines on the ruler and the mat; slide the ruler to the raw edge; place your hand firmly on the ruler and slice the edge straight with the cutter.

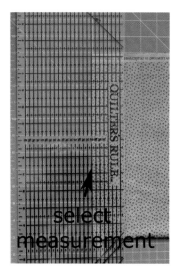

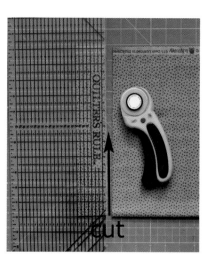

3. Turn the fabric and replace the fabric on the right side of the cutting mat with the neatly cut edge on the left-hand side. Put the ruler on the left. Slide the ruler on to the fabric until the desired measurement is reached, i.e. the ruler covers the required amount of fabric to be cut.

Fab **R** ic on the right
Ru **L** er on the left.

(Left-handed students ignore the above - your ruler moves across the material from the Right)

4. Hold the ruler steady with your hand and firmly push the cutter blade away from you up the side of the ruler.

Sewing Machines

All the techniques in this book can be created without a machine; it just takes a little longer!

There is no need for anything more advanced than a basic hand or electric model. Hopefully, you can sew a straight line with a medium stitch length - 10 stitches per inch (4 stitches per cm). The straight stitch presser foot is ideal for most of the techniques; a zipper foot would be useful for fine tucks, piping and inserting zips. Pin Tucks need a special presser foot (page 24).

If you do possess a sewing machine, keeping it lightly oiled and free from fluff will prolong its life, cut down on servicing costs and improve the performance. My machines have a lot of use, so they are cleaned and oiled most weeks, but if you do not use the machine a tremendous amount, it need not be attended to so frequently, i.e. a little more than once in a blue moon!! A routine maintenance at the end of a long project is ideal; clean the dust out, oil the moving parts, but...

OIL ONLY WHERE RECOMMENDED IN THE INSTRUCTION BOOK

Running the machine fast afterwards will allow the fine oil to lubricate all the moving parts and it will be ready for the next project.

Use a medium size of needle (80/12) when you are sewing with medium weight fabric; a finer needle (70/10) for lightweight fabrics; for applying frills, backs to cushions and/or heavy weight materials, it is advantageous to use a large needle (100/16). Needles should always be straight and sharp; they blunt with time and use, so change them frequently. Be careful that the tip is intact or it could snag the work and the machine will seem to be hammering or tapping more than normal.

Most threads are suitable for use in the sewing machine, ranging from polyesters to mercerised cottons. Sewing machines appear to prefer the same type and make of thread on the top spool and in the bobbin. Although - invisible thread should only be used on the top spool with a cotton or polyester thread underneath.

Sometimes changing the threads can upset the tension on the machine. If the top thread is lying on the surface and not locked evenly into the lower thread, you have to slacken the tension on the top thread.

On the front of the machine, there is a dial, with either a (+) or (-), or a series of numbers from 1 to 10; normally the indicator line will be approximately in the centre of the dial, but to slacken the top tension, turn the dial to the (-) or a lower number. This allows the top thread to run more freely, interlocking with the lower thread in a uniform manner. Should the reverse situation be apparent, with lower thread lying tautly and not locked correctly into the top thread, the tension dial should be turned to a higher number or towards the (+).

Some makes of machine have a sewing table attachment; this is useful for supporting the work and provides a space for the left hand while guiding the material.

Finding The Seam Allowance on the Machine

The usual S/A recommended in many patchwork and quilting books is ¼"(0.65 - 0.75cm). This is an adequate width for accurate piecing of points and joining of junctions when sewing two layers together. Most sewing machines have a special ¼" foot that you can attach - often referred to as a 'patchwork foot'. You may have one amongst your presser feet or they can be purchased.

Alternatively attach your regular presser foot and try moving the needle position to achieve the selected S/A. Sewing machines with a swing needle (moves from side to side) often have a series of different settings for the needle position in relation to the edge of the presser foot. Frequently, in the straight stitch setting, the needle can be shifted by altering the stitch width setting or shifting the needle position using a separate dial, knob or button. On many Janome models, if you adjust the stitch width setting to 5.5 (when in straight stitch mode) the needle will move to ¼" from the right-hand edge of the regular presser foot. This ability to move the needle and set it at this distance from the right-hand side of the presser foot is advantageous as the regular presser foot can be used. The regular foot has a wide slot unlike the patchwork foot that only has a narrow hole. It is remarkably easy to forget that you have the patchwork foot attached and select a decorative pattern then... Whack... The needle breaks. This may upset the timing on your sewing machine if it happens frequently. The other advantage of using the regular foot and not the patchwork one is that the regular foot sits properly on the feed dogs. Quite a lot of patchwork feet do not cover the feed dogs properly so you don't get the full pulling power of the feed dogs against the base of the presser foot. (For those who don't know what feed dogs are - read your instruction book!)

If you choose to alter the needle position and set the needle ¼" from the right-hand edge of the presser foot, check the measurement with an accurate ruler (tape-measures aren't that accurate), and make a note of the setting.

Sometimes in this book a $^3/_8$" (1cm) S/A is chosen. This wider S/A is selected when piecing a seam consisting of multiple layers of fabric, as all the raw edges may not be accurately aligned. (With a bit of luck and fingers crossed, all layers will be caught in this larger seam.) Do not panic, selecting a different S/A is not difficult. Use the standard presser foot and look on the throat plate (metal plate beneath).

On older sewing machines, $^3/_8$" (1cm) is often marked on the throat plate. Metric machines may have the plate printed in centimetres or millimetres; consequently 1cm will be displayed as 1 or 10 (10mm = 1cm). Imperial machines (often older models) frequently have their throat plates marked in eighths so $^3/_8$" is easy to find. Alternatively, move the needle from its central position towards the left-hand side of the presser foot (away from the main body of machine). On most machines the needle will now be $^3/_8$" (1cm) away from the right-hand edge of the presser foot. Many modern models have several needle positions, check which position provides an accurate S/A.

If there is no possible method of moving the needle nor can a ¼" patchwork foot be purchased, try sticking a piece of masking tape to the body of the sewing machine, setting it at the desired seam allowance from the needle. Machines that are supplied with a narrow hem foot only and machines with large presser feet will benefit from this trick.

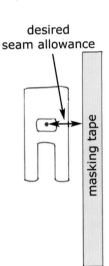

desired
seam allowance

masking tape

As a last resort, you can rule the seam allowance on to the fabric using a hard sharp pencil and sew along the pencil line.

Choice of Fabrics for 'Tucks, Textures & Pleats'

Calico

Calico is a plain woven cotton cloth, sometimes bleached, mainly sold in Britain in an unbleached state. It is distinguished by the dark fleck of fibrous cotton that occurs intermittently. Sometimes loomstate (cloth prior to any refining process) calico has coloured threads caught in the weave. The name calico originates from Calcutta Cloth, from the Indian city that initially exported it.

In America, calico is a printed cloth, with a figured pattern and they refer to British calico as muslin. This can cause confusion as muslin in England is a fine loose weave, certainly not suitable for most of the techniques in this book.

Calico varies from supplier to supplier. You will find an assortment of different weights, weaves and colours. Use a medium weight cloth with a firm weave. The finer weaves do not support the pleats and folds involved in some of the designs. Thick weaves are often too rigid to twist easily. Some fabrics have a fire resistant dressing applied to the surface; the dressing may make the material too stiff for use in textured work.

A further advantage of calico is the cost. It is relatively inexpensive compared to other materials; consequently, you can use it with gay abandon and really explore all the exciting and innovative ideas found in this book.

Washing Calico

Most of the samples that are shown in the photographs are made from unwashed calico. The fabric has not been washed as the manufacturers' dressings stiffen the material and I find the stiffened fabric easier to manipulate. Your hands may go up in horror at this flagrant disobedience of all the rules, but if you choose to wash the calico beforehand, it can be difficult to remove all the creases with the iron. Try pressing the material when damp and avoid using a hot iron as this may singe the surface. Should the fabric prove very difficult to iron flat then try placing damp material in the deep-freeze for thirty minutes before pressing.

To wash the cloth successfully - hand-wash in warm water, cool rinse, remove the excess water by rolling the fabric in a towel; tumble it until almost dry and if essential, lightly press. If the article is a cushion, push the pillow/pad (feather or polyester) inside before tumbling on a medium heat, remove when almost dry, either "air" in the airing/drying cupboard or toss it on the sofa, and do not rest the weary head until it has dried properly! If a tumble-dryer is not part of the household equipment, still replace the pillow/pad into the wet soggy cover as this will keep the cover in shape while drying.

Calico cushions do need washing and in my house that is not often; after all who wants to spend time laundering when one can play with another tucking technique?

Other Types of Fabrics

Textured effects look equally interesting in other plain materials, hand dyes or small self-patterned prints. Chintz (glazed cotton) creates attractive areas of light and shadow due to the sheen on the cloth from the glazing. Chintz can become limp after washing, as the glaze washes off; apparently there are no products that restore the surface.

There is a wide choice of fabrics on the market from gabardines, light-weight denims, sateens, satins, tickings, cretonnes and silks. All of these can be used for textured creations.

A simple tucked cushion will be totally different in another type of cloth.

Trumpet Cushion & Somerset inserts in chintz and furnishing fabric (two triangles sewn together form the Trumpets): Sue Wood
Silk Confirmation Dress with Bias tucks: Lesley Seddon

To Rip or not to Rip

Tearing fabric is not a good idea. If you rip the material, the edge will be stretched and damaged. In my opinion, you should only tear when you wish to fray the edge.

When cloth is ripped, it tears along the weft thread. If the weft thread is not aligned parallel to the selvedge (a frequent occurrence in the modern mechanical weaving process); the tear could then be a slanting line. We have all experienced trying to re-align the material - so be kind, cut the cloth, don't rip it!

Choice of Threads

As discussed in the section on machines, most threads can be used. Matching coloured thread to the material will maximise the textural effect and disguise any mistakes. Contrasting threads may add a colourful dimension to the design, but any deviation from the chosen path will show!

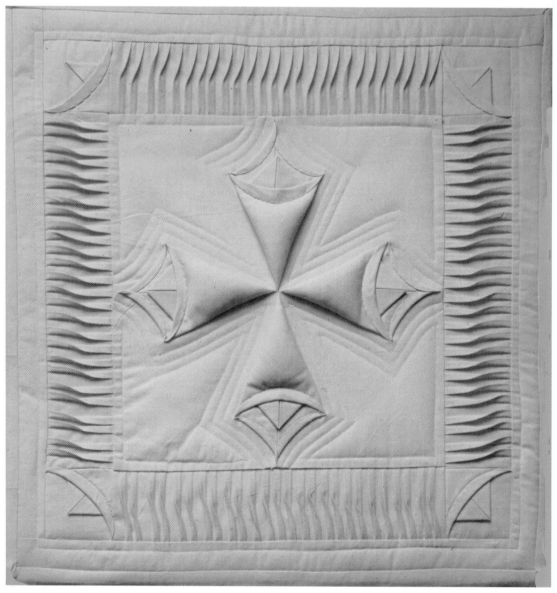

Tucks and Trumpets 20" square. Created from calico: Jennie Rayment

Thread Savers

An invaluable device that saves yards and yards of thread. It is really a method of continuous sewing, rather like chain piecing in patchwork. (This is not my own idea - it's an old tailoring trick.)

Rummage in the trash bin and find a small scrap of unwanted fabric. At the end of any line of stitching, DO NOT lift the presser foot, DO NOT remove the work or cut the threads but continue to sew. Sew off the work on to this scrap of material and STOP on the scrap. The presser foot is now sitting on the scrap of material. Leave the scrap there - do not move it.

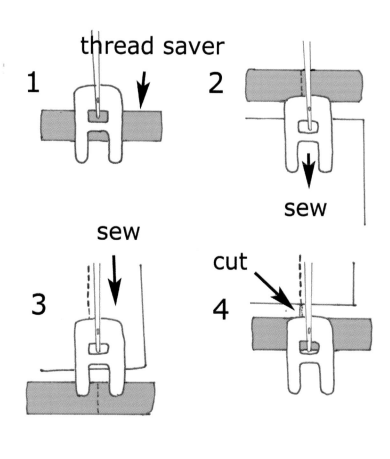

Detach the work from the small scrap by cutting the threads immediately <u>behind</u> (at the back) the presser foot (between the scrap and the work).

Continue with the next set of seams. Sew off the scrap and down the next seam (scrap is now attached to the beginning of the seam). At the end of this line of stitching, cut the scrap off from the beginning and replace it in front of the presser foot. Sew from the main piece of work on to the scrap again. Cut threads behind the presser foot. Repeat, repeat, repeat etc.!

This scrap is called a Thread Saver and will save a vast amount of thread - no long dangling ends; it prevents tangled threads at the start of the seam; threads snag less often in the bottom bobbin; the needle does not unthread inadvertently because the threads were cut too short, and it's energy saving - no need to raise the presser foot. Finally, for those who habitually deviate at the end of a seam, it may keep you on the straight and narrow - try it. It may help.

Give the idea a whirl - it seems complicated but is very easy when you get the hang of it. A further advantage of this natty notion occurs when you commence sewing on a thick material or begin stitching with the zipper foot; the material feeds more easily under the presser foot as it is already sitting on a fabric surface, i.e. the Thread Saver.

Remember: The only place to cut the threads is behind the presser foot (once you have sewn on to the Thread Saver and have stopped on that scrap).

Tucks and Pleats

Inspiration from natural to man-made sources abounds when you cast an eye around. Any series of parallel lines or ridges can be used as a basis for the initial tucked effect.

Nature is brimming with ideas for tucks or pleats - there being very little difference in my opinion as both involve folds in the fabric although tucks are stitched in place whereas pleats are merely folded over and sewn at both ends. The underside of mushrooms, the crags in rocks, ploughed lines in fields, bark of knarled trees; some fruits and vegetables have ridged surfaces that could be translated into tucks. Landscapes and seascapes lend themselves to distorted and curvaceous tuck formations. Have you ever seen straight waves?

Investigate your environment. Look at roof structures, staircases, scaffolding, tiles, aerial photographs, roads, railway tracks, bridges. Contemporary art and sculpture can display a linear format that may be expanded. We are surrounded by lines in different patterns and arrangements which would all make starting points for your design, then you can alter these patterns by flexing the tucks in different directions.

From art to architecture, sea to sky, ancient modern, there is a wealth of creativity from the harmonious to the abstract.

Remember the golden rule:

'MISTAKES DO NOT MATTER, THE RESULT IS JUST DIFFERENT'

Tucked Cushion & Tucked Cushion with Trumpets: Jennie Rayment

As all this choice can be unsettling, I have suggested certain measurements and seam allowances for a panel of tucks, hoping that when you have experimented with the technique you will gain the confidence to play and discover new ideas for yourself.

How to Start The Tucks

Sewing a series of tucks along an edge will reduce the original width of the fabric, to form a square it is necessary to cut a rectangle of material. The width of the rectangle will depend on the quantity and size of the tucks. Tucks will lie more easily if you sew down the straight grain of the material (parallel to the selvedges) rather than across it. Matching thread colour to the material disguises unintentional mistakes.

To make a panel approximately 12½" (31cm) square:

1. Cut a piece of fabric 26" x 12½" (66cm x 31cm) deep. (The depth being down the selvedge.)

2. Use a pencil or fine fabric marker to mark measurements along the top long side of the strip of fabric.

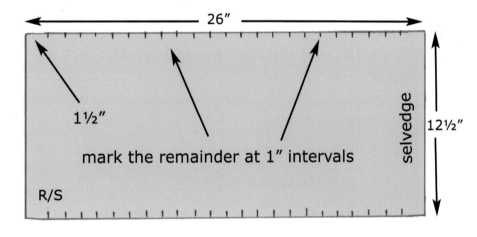

Start 1½" (4cm) from left-hand edge then mark the remainder of the side at 1" (2.5cm) intervals. Repeat the marks at the same distances along the lower edge. It is unnecessary to rule lines down the fabric as the pencil marks cannot be easily removed.

3. Thread the machine with matching thread on the top and bottom spool, and start stitching. Fold the fabric on the first set of marks, and sew along the fold. Sew from **A** to **B**.

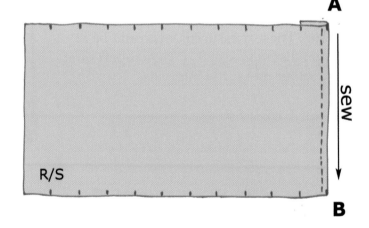

Running the edge of the presser foot down the fold will help keep the width of the tuck accurate. Some machines have several needle settings, and you can re-position the needle nearer to or further from the edge of the presser foot to change the width of the tuck making it wider or narrower. Life should be easy and not like hard work - use the edge of the presser foot and keep it on the fold. Aim for approximately ¼" (0.75cm) S/A.

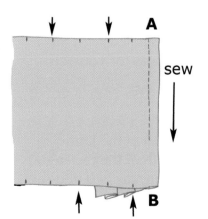

4. Fold and sew down on every set of pencil marks.

Try to sew up one way and down the other; if the sewing is only done from one direction, the sample will distort. When lines of stitch are constantly sewn in the same direction i.e. top **A** to bottom **B**, the presser foot drags the fibres slightly each time, consequently pulling the material out of shape. By commencing sewing from **A** towards **B**, turning work and sewing next seam from **B** to **A**, the fibres will be less distorted.

Remember to use a Thread Saver! At the end of each line of stitching sew on to the Saver, cutting the threads between the tucked panel and the Thread Saver at the back of the presser foot (see page 13).

Do not start or finish the tucks too close to the sides; leave space for a seam allowance for the border.

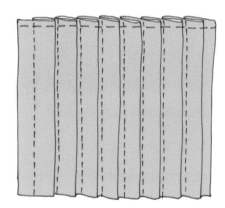

5. Press all the tucks in one direction. Stitch along the top side securing all the pleats; use ¼" (0.75cm) S/A (seam allowance).

6. Using a pencil or a marking pen, mark even measurements down the side of the panel. These measurements could be at equal distances e.g. 3" (7.5cm) apart or at any other measured intervals.

← ¼"
↕ 3"
↕ 3"
↕ 3"
↕ 3"
← ¼"

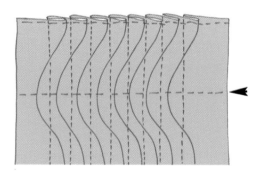

7. Turn the work and on the next measured mark sew a second line parallel to the first line, twisting the tucks over as you go (the tucks lie in the opposite direction).

Sew across the work on each marked measurement flexing the tucks in alternate directions to create a wave pattern. Finally sew close to the lower edge to stabilise the pleats.

16

Use a small wooden barbecue/kebab skewer, point of stitch ripper or fine-pointed scissors to help turn each tuck and hold it down while sewing. Fingers are not always nimble enough to hold the fabric precisely where needed, and a machine needle through the finger is best avoided.

Developing the Theme

Try sewing diagonally across the work twisting the tucks in different directions. Do all the tucks have to go in the same direction? What about twisting the tucks in pairs, pushing two towards each other on one line, then alternate the effect on the next row of stitching? This explanation might help:

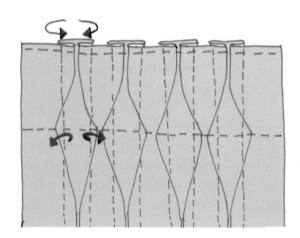

Make an even number of tucks. Divide the work into pairs of tucks or let's call them 'couples' of tucks. A very common couple that we all understand is Mummy and Daddy; divide the tucks into sets of Mummies and Daddies. As you sew across the edge of the tucked panel, twist each Mummy so that she 'kisses' each Daddy (marital harmony). Alternatively, Mummy puts her arms around Daddy (tucks overlap); that's real lovey-doveyiness! BUT when it comes to sewing the next row, our happy couples have an enormous row and turn away from each other and go in the opposite direction. Mummy will now kiss the man next door! Will divorce be the next step?

Fortunately, when it comes to the third row, all our unhappy couples make it up and Mummy kisses Daddy again as they did on the first row. This pattern of marital harmony and divorce continues all the way down the material.

This makes an interesting honeycomb pattern, and depending on the initial depth of tucks sewn, fascinating areas of light and shadow appear.

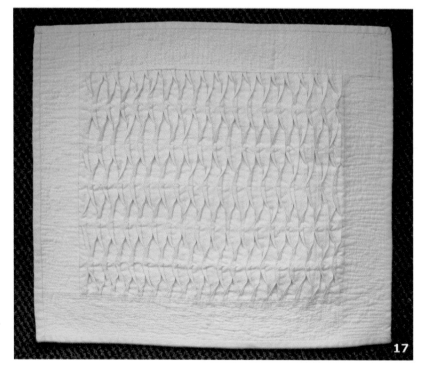

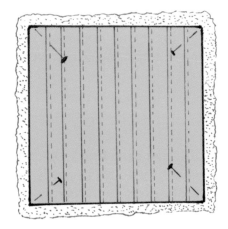

Try sewing curved lines across the material representing a wave design, or maybe to disguise some misshapen tucks. You do not have to sew straight - wiggles work well!

Placing the tucked fabric on to wadding/batting before you start twisting the tucks will remove some of the buckling of the material. This will also quilt the work and anchor the surface. Pin the piece to the wadding (batting) in each corner before starting.

Change the measurements between the lines of tucks as you flex the tucks in opposite directions. If the lines of stitching are too close then tucks will not lie absolutely flat and the fabric may distort. Does it matter? Experiment with the effect.

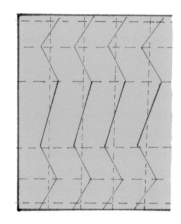

Extend the ideas into a panel, positioning sections with tucks flexed in different ways. Use the design for a headboard, wall-hanging, section of a quilt, part of a jacket or waistcoat. This technique is most effective for an impressive tie-back and cushions in abundance.

Why not sew random tucks with distorted folds to create the bark on trees or a geological formation? Quilt the resulting creation on some wadding for additional texture.

Experiment with striped fabrics, sewing down or across the stripes. This is really easy as sewing down the edges of the stripes will keep the sewing straight!

Tucked Cushion made with striped material: Jennie Rayment

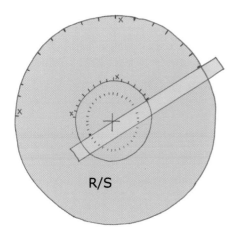

R/S

Circles can be most effective

Cut a large circle of material and mark the centre. Set the point of a compass on this dot and draw a smaller circle. Line up the midpoint of a protractor with the centre and mark every 9°, 10° or 15° intervals. Align a ruler with each degree mark and draw a corresponding mark on the inner and outer circle edge.

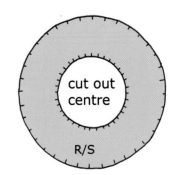

cut out centre

R/S

It pays to put **X**'s in various places so that you can check the tucks are made on the correct sets of marks. If you reach a set of **X**'s and they are not aligned for that particular tuck then it is probable that the fabric was not folded on the corresponding marks at some point.

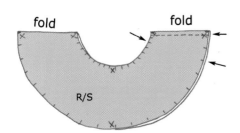

fold   fold

R/S

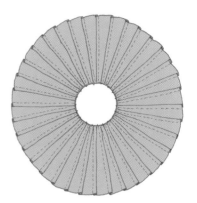

Cut out the inner circle before folding the fabric on each set of marks and sew tucks, using ¼" (0.75cm) S/A. Remember to alternate the stitching direction as you sew each tuck.

On completion press all the tucks in the same direction and cover the hole in the centre before commencing a little tuck twisting! (For a more detailed explanation on tucking a circle see 'Tucks & Textures Two'.)

To make this wall-hanging, cut one 30" (75cm) diameter circle and draw a 10" (25cm) diameter inner circle. Clearly mark the fabric at 9° intervals (making 40 marks). Use ¼" (0.75cm) S/A to make the tucks.

Tucked Circle edged in Prairie Points with a 'Bow Tie' appliquéed in the centre: Jennie Rayment

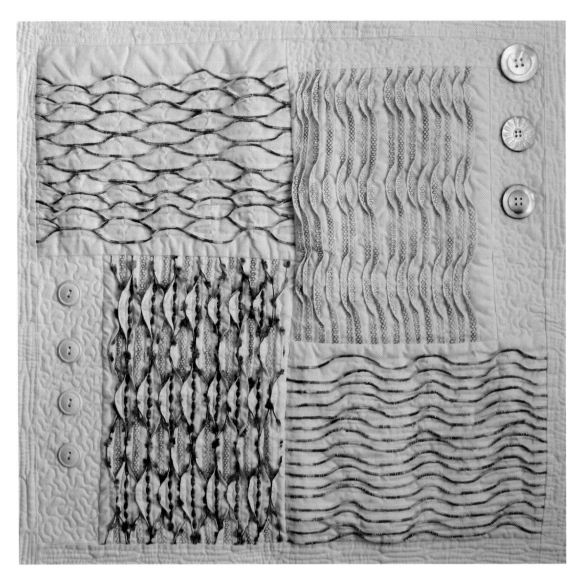

Embellishing the Tucks

Why not decorate the tucks with machine stitching? Use a decorative stitch to secure the twisted tucks and/or stitch between the rows of tucks before twisting. Test the stitch design first, as some intricate patterns do not reproduce accurately on uneven surfaces. A braid or thick thread could be applied between each row before doing any twisting or over the tucks after they have been twisted for added decorative effect.

What about satin-stitching along the tuck edge with a variegated/multicoloured thread before twisting? Use the satin stitch (zigzag pattern) on your machine to cover the edge of the tuck and create a line of colour.

1. Thread top and bottom bobbin with a variegated thread. Insert a fine needle 9 - 10 (60 - 70) into the machine.

2. Set the stitch width at the maximum size that your machine will produce, set the stitch length at the satin stitch setting (approximately 0.6 - 0.4). Attach the appliqué/satin stitching foot (the presser foot with a cut away channel on the underside - the channel allows the foot to pass evenly over any dense decorative stitch without jamming on the raised stitching). If possible use a presser foot with an open front.

3. Test the stitch settings along the folded edge of a scrap of material. Ensure that you achieve a solid line of dense stitching.

4. Set the folded edge of the tuck just inside the left-hand edge of the presser foot. The needle will catch the edge of the fabric with the left-hand side of the zigzag; the right-hand side will pass right over the edge of the material. Begin the stitching a short distance from the edge of the material otherwise the fabric will not feed through easily and may jam underneath the presser foot.

Run the machine fast, an inconsistent speed can produce an uneven stitch appearance. Let your hands guide the material through, do not pull or push. Pulling or pushing the material will lengthen the stitch width. Be careful not to retard the material, i.e. hang on too tightly - this will cause the stitch to jam and the only remedy is to stop, undo the snarled lump and start again. P.S. It pays to check the bottom bobbin after stitching half the tucks as it is irritating if the thread runs out halfway down the next edge.

5. On completion, press the fabric with all the tucks in the same direction and twist as described earlier in this chapter

Troubleshooting

a. If the stitching keeps jamming, slacken the pressure off the presser foot to allow the foot to pass more easily over the raised stitching. (This only applies if your machine has a foot pressure regulator, see the instruction book.) Alternatively lengthen the stitch length slightly and have a less solid appliquéed line.

b. Should the appliqué thread keep breaking, increase the needle size - use a higher number such as 12 - 14 (80 - 90).

c. Any little gaps in the solid line of satin stitching can always be concealed by careful colouring over the gap with a fine felt tip pen.

It has to be said that some machines do not do a very effective job even after trying all the above tips and techniques so why not appliqué a yarn or textured thread to the edge of the tuck instead. This gives a similarly interesting effect without so much aggravation and may prove faster to apply. There are some fabulous yarns available nowadays in the wool and craft shops.

Appliquéing yarn to the edge of the tucks

Once again set the widest zigzag width on your sewing machine but this time keep the stitch length at the regular stitch length setting (approximately 2mm).

1. Fill the top and bottom spool with the same colour as the appliqué yarn. For those who prefer nylon filament (invisible thread) thread the top or bottom spool with the filament and use cotton thread in preference to polyester on the other. It is inadvisable to use nylon filament on both spools, as the machine may not sew properly. In addition, when using this type of thread on the bottom bobbin, wind it on at a slow speed.

2. Position the tucked fabric just underneath the left-hand side of the presser foot. Lay the yarn alongside the tuck. Start the zigzag by sewing into the very edge of the tucked fabric, zigzag over the yarn and back into the edge of the material. Keep going until you reach the end of the tuck.

Putting a tiny amount of stress on the yarn and keeping it at a slight angle to the tucked edge will help to keep the yarn on the edge of the fabric. If possible sew up and down the lines of tucks to prevent the fabric distorting. On occasions it may be more efficient to work in the same direction, if the material distorts, realign with a good tug. Should any section of the appliquéed yarn not be caught by the stitching, re-stitch that section where relevant.

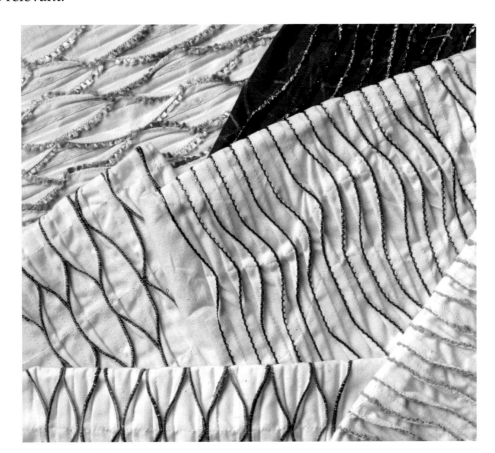

Zipper Foot Tucks and Pin Tucks

Zipper Foot Tucks

You have seen how easy it is to use the normal presser foot to create wide pleats. Now try using the zipper foot to produce narrow tucks similar to pin tucks. (Pin tucks are so called because they are the height of a pin.)

Glancing around, your immediate surroundings contain many objects with fine lines that would make an excellent design source for a series of zipper foot tucks, e.g. stripes in tartan fabrics and wallpapers; ridges in stone and pottery; rocky cracks, crags and crazy paving plus wrinkles of all description!

Why try to be creative when the world around us is teeming with designs for us to interpret in our own way, although you may choose to conjure up a few ideas of your own?

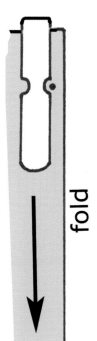

fold

Creating a Zipper Foot Tuck

Put the zipper foot on the machine and move the needle to the right-hand side. Fold the fabric. Position the zipper foot beside the edge of the fabric fold. The width of the tuck will be determined by the distance the needle is placed from the fold.

Start with the presser foot set completely on the beginning of the material. Sometimes a narrow zipper foot doesn't feed the fabric through properly unless the foot is sitting completely on top of the fabric.

Sew along the fold to the end of the fabric in an orderly fashion, re-fold the material in a different direction and sew another tuck.

Explore the effect of tucks stitched in an organised format or experiment with an abstract fashion, possibly stitching tucks over tucks.

Hand Sewers: Use a small back-stitch or a small running stitch. Sew close to the edge of the fabric fold.

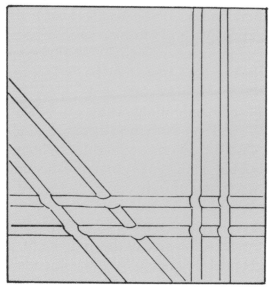

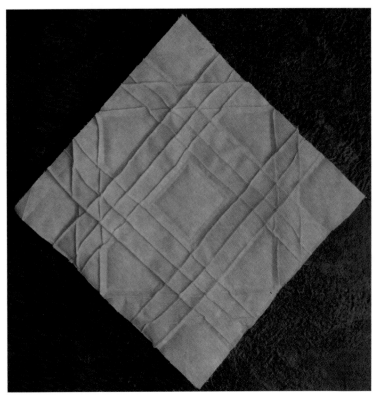

Placing the tucked section on to wadding (batting) and adding some quilting between the tucks will emphasise the texture.

Random tucks make marvellous mountainous regions for a landscape. Turn the work over and look at the back, the wrong side may be more interesting than the right side. Why not combine both aspects in the same sample?

Pin Tucks

To produce pin tucks, a special presser foot is required, and it is rare for this to be standard issue in the attachments provided with the sewing machine. In addition, a twin needle has to be used in conjunction with two reels of thread - one thread through each needle.

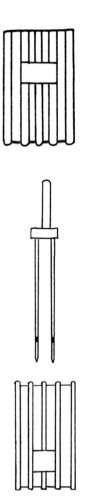

There are several different types of pin tuck feet to choose from; the amount of grooves determines the size and spacing of the tucks. Check when you purchase a pin tuck foot that you are sold the correct sized twin needle. The two needles should fit between the grooves on the underside of the foot.

Attach the pin tuck foot to the machine and insert the twin needle. Check that the neck of the needle is correctly positioned (a twin needle is expensive, and can snap easily if incorrectly placed). Thread up with two evenly sized and equally weighted spools of similar thread; on the top of the machine, there may be two spindles - one for each thread, if not place the spools in tandem on the single spindle. On occasions, a carefully positioned knitting needle can be slotted into or taped on to the machine to create an extra thread spindle. (Failing to have two equally sized reels, wind thread on two machine bobbins and use these instead. Put one bobbin on the individual thread spindles or put them both together on the horizontal/upright one.)

If your machine has a tension dial with a central metal ring, drop one thread either side of this ring; if not, place both threads through the normal channel. Try not to twist the threads before threading the needles.

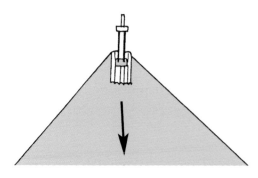

Finally tighten up the top thread tension, i.e. turn to a higher number or towards the (+) sign. This makes the pin tuck more pronounced.

Place the fabric completely underneath the presser foot. It is preferable to stitch quite slowly as the twin needles are fragile. Sewing across the diagonal/bias of the fabric gives a marginally better raised effect than stitching along the straight grain.

A thin cord can be placed underneath the material, and the grooves in the foot will guide it through. It helps to hold the end of the cord as you start. Ensure that the cord remains in the centre of the foot or it can slip out and will not be enclosed in the tuck.

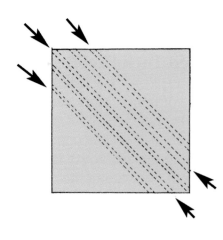

Now, sit at your sewing machine and get thoroughly bored with trundling up and down making pin tucks. Remember to alternate the direction of the stitching to prevent the material distorting. Keeping the tucks straight is easy as one of the grooves in the pin tuck foot can be aligned with the previous tuck. Just check that it remains in the same groove and the lines will be perfect!

Intriguing and fascinating patterns can be created using curved or random tucks or sections of straight tucks at different angles. Why not create a large piece of pin tucked fabric, cut it up and use the sections for patchwork?

Inserting panels of pin tucks into cushions, quilts, head-boards, tie-backs and garments will add an interesting textural touch. Experiment with different coloured threads (one through each needle) to add a bit more pizzazz.

But if you do not possess a pin tuck foot, twin needles can be used for decorative effect. Fine parallel lines in contrasting coloured threads look delightful. You can even have zigzag lines if you adjust the stitch width. Do not adjust the stitch width by more than half the maximum distance indicated on the stitch width dial/knob/button on your machine, or one of the needles will hit the presser foot and break.

Pin & Regular Tucks in a spiral Log Cabin design: Jennie Rayment

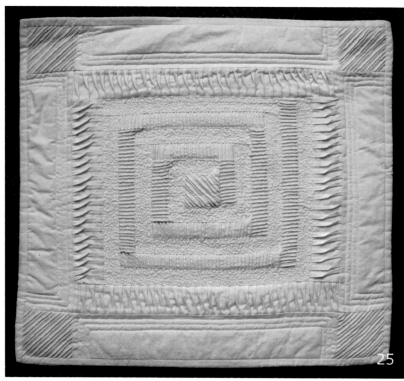

Crossing Over the Tucks

As explained in the previous chapters, a variety of different ways of tucking and pleating fabric have been developed in the course of my explorations into the world of fabric manipulation. One of my students, Angie Mckimm, was experimenting with one of these ideas, and discovered the exciting possibilities of tucking across previously constructed pleats.

I have expanded this concept and created a large panel. This technique is quick to produce, looks most attractive and has lots of potential design possibilities that could be explored ad infinitum.

Technically, it helps to be accurate with the measuring of the tucks, but who knows what exciting textural effects you may inadvertently discover if you don't measure accurately?

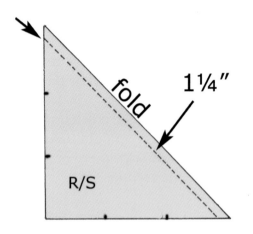

Constructing a Crossed Tuck Panel

1. Cut a 24″ (60cm) square of fabric. Mark each edge at 8″ (20cm) intervals on R/S.

2. Fold the fabric on the diagonal (R/S out). Draw a line 1¼″ (3cm) from the fold. Sew along the drawn line. Take care not to stretch the material as it is on the bias.

3. Fold the fabric diagonally on each set of marks either side of the central seam. Draw a line 1¼″ (3cm) from the fold, sew along the drawn line. Five large tucks are formed running across the fabric.

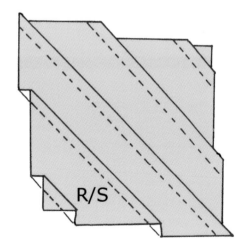

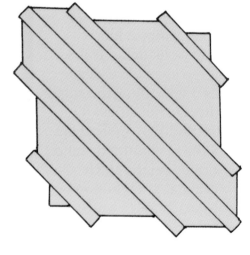

4. Press the tucks even and flat over the seam. Inserting a narrow ruler, flat slat or a couple of knitting needles will help to get the tucks pressed equidistantly over the seam.

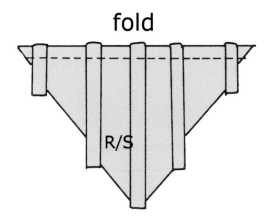

fold

R/S

5. Fold the pressed square on the other diagonal. Measure 1¼" (3cm) from the fold, draw a line and sew along the drawn line. Repeat on the remaining marks to create five stitched tucks. Press all the tucks flat. The work should resemble a diagonal lattice approximately 15" (38cm) square.

6. Square up the panel as it may have distorted in the sewing. Straighten the edges carefully as the flattened tucks are bulky and they may be difficult to cut through.

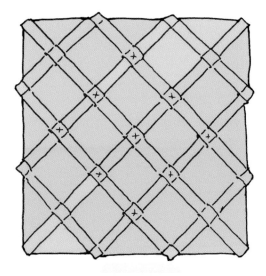

7. Press the panel well. Secure the junctions of the tucks with a few stitches to keep the folds stable.

Alternatively, embellish these junctions with tassels, buttons, beads, French knots, Bullion knots, pom-poms, cross-stitching or use a quilting tie of some description. Why not use a contrasting coloured thread to the fabric?

Complete the panel with a border to make an interesting and innovative cushion or inset the panel into a quilt, incorporate it into a garment or utilise as the centre section of a wall-hanging or headboard.

P.S. A quilting tie is not complicated. By hand, sew through all the layers leaving a long thread end at the start of the sewing on the R/S; make another complete stitch through all the layers and finish on the R/S leaving another long thread end. Knot both long ends together with a reef knot or tie in a firm bow on the R/S of the material. Simples!

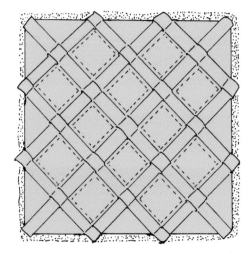

Extending the Technique

Place the completed panel on wadding and a backing fabric and quilt in the space between the tucks.

Roll the edges of the tucks and insert scraps of material under the folds.

Make the tucks straight across the original square at right angles to the edges forming a 'Noughts and Crosses' design. Why not embroider 0 and X in the spaces?

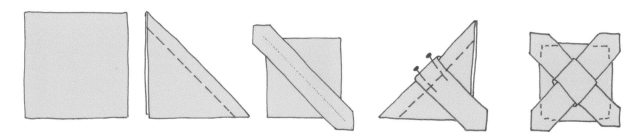

Alternatively play it simple - cut a square and make one fat tuck across the diagonal; flatten and make another equal sized tuck from the opposite corner. Easy-peasy!

Now you have seen how to create the Crossing Over the Tucks design, experiment with this technique across a different shape, e.g. hexagon or octagon; Angie's original idea came from an octagonal shape. Investigate the effect of three tucks across a triangle, or six tucks across a hexagon, and so on. Go on - have a play!

**Like so many of these textural ideas,
the possibilities are limitless - all you need is time!**

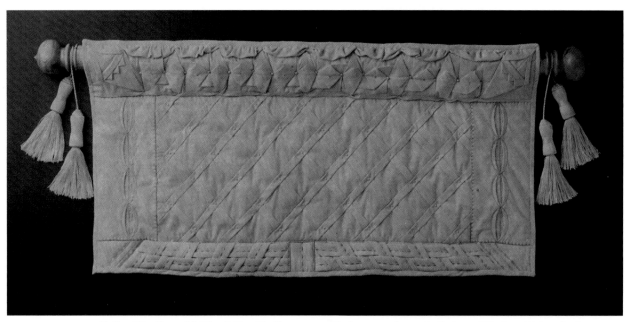

Calico Headboard 20" x 36" with Cross over Tucks central panel. Origami Twists, Triangle Cornets, Bias strips and weaving combined to make the border: Shelagh Jarvis

Ruched and Gathered Textures

Not only can you tuck fabric but it can be gathered. Imagine the scrunched up effect of tiny pebbles, the hide of an elderly elephant, or the nasty puckering of cellulite - cottage cheese bottoms! I must not put you off as, in all honesty, ruched material has a most attractive appearance.

Use of gathering techniques can create a smocked illusion; insert fine sections of ruching to produce a seer-sucker type of material; panels of 'smocking' could be incorporated into fashion garments, cushions, tie-backs and pelmets. Can you visualise the ruched and textured facade of a pelmet?

Ruched frills can be added to cushions, curtains, clothing and edges of small cot quilts. Different effects will be created by employing the bias or straight grain of the fabric.

Ruched Inset

1. Cut a long 2″ (5cm) strip of fabric. Select the longest stitch length on the machine or use a large hand running stitch, and sew down one long edge.

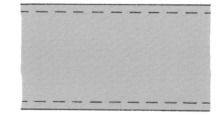

Tightening up the top stitch tension on the machine (turn to a higher number or towards the +) will help with the gathering. (Snapping thread or excessive gathering is caused by over-tightening the tension.)

2. Repeat on the opposite edge, then draw up the threads; the top thread is already tighter due to the adjusted tension and can be pulled easily. Be careful not to pull so hard that the other end comes through! Continue gathering up until you have decided that there is sufficient ruching.

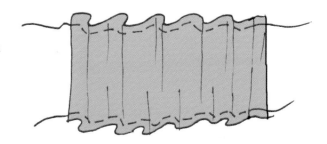

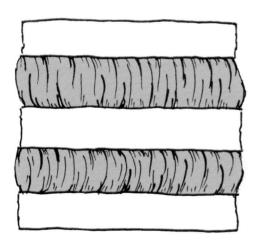

This strip can now be inserted into your work, with plain un-gathered sections either side for a pleasing textured effect.

Why not cut wider strips and experiment with several lines of gathering at equal intervals or see what happens if you sew random lines spaced unevenly apart? Secure the gathered layers with a wide satin stitch, in a contrasting thread colour. You could gather in a curved or undulating manner, depicting waves and the froth on the beach. Just play!

29

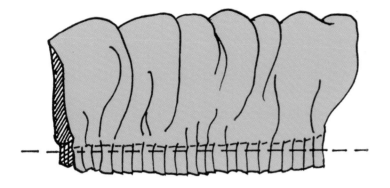

Ruched Frill

For a ruched frill, fold the gathered strip in half and stitch along the edge.

Add this to the edge of cushions and curtains for an attractive and unusual finish.

Cutting the strip on the straight grain of the fabric produces a more sharply defined appearance to the edge of the frill as opposed to cutting the fabric on the bias which creates a more rounded effect.

Ruched Fabric

This looks absolutely stunning, but I must warn you that until you add a border to the sample, the result resembles that piece of prized work that you screwed up and discarded in disgust!

1. Cut a large square of light-medium weight fabric - ruching reduces the total area by four, i.e. 16" (40cm) square could end up as a 4" (10cm) square.

2. Select a thread that matches the colour of the fabric. Use this thread on the top spool and in the bottom bobbin. Set the machine for the longest stitch length. (If your machine has a basting facility use this instead - select the smaller basting length). Tighten the top thread tension slightly.

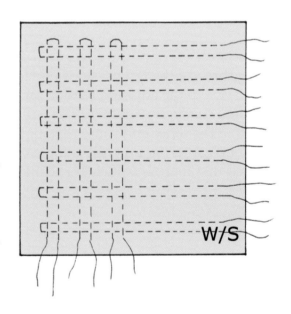

3. Start with the W/S of the material uppermost. Follow the pattern shown in the diagram:

Start a short distance in from the edge, sew across the fabric. Stop - do not break the thread. Turn the work and re-position the foot approximately ½" (1.25cm) away from the first line of stitching (jump across). Sew back to the beginning of the first line of stitching and break the threads. The stitching forms an elongated 'U' shape.

4. Repeat this manoeuvre until you have covered all the fabric. Follow the same technique, stitch across the previously sewn lines. A stitched grid is produced.

3. When all the stitching is complete, hold the fabric firmly, pull up all the top threads; these threads lie on the W/S of the material, be careful, as they may break if you tug too hard.

DO NOT pull the threads on the R/S (from the bottom bobbin) at the same time because the stitching will lock in place and nothing will happen.

Draw up one set of threads down one side entirely, then draw up the adjacent side. Arrange the gathers so they are evenly distributed.

4. To prevent everything from unravelling, it is advisable to stitch the ruched square on to a piece of backing fabric. Pin this indescribably scrumpled piece on a larger square of fabric, and firmly sew round the sides flattening the puckered edges as you go.

5. Cut strips of fabric for the borders. By adding these to opposite sides first, then opening out and adding longer strips to the remaining sides, the bordering will be easy.

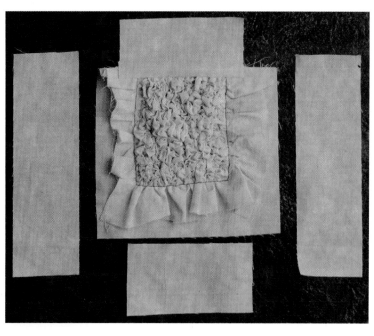

Now you can admire it, and I suspect that you will agree that until the borders are added, your sample did look a mess! A few seed pearls could be sewn on the ruching, resembling glistening dew drops.

How about a ruched panel with bead work on an evening bag, placed on a box lid or made from silk forming the centre of a fabulous cushion as a wedding present? Why not make the middle of a circular design from scrunched material?

Ric-Rac Frill

Ric-Rac is an undulating woven ribbon that can be used to decorate any edge, conceal seam joins, enhance plain areas; the Seminole Indians applied it to the bands in between their strip patchwork designs.

The same effect can be achieved by folding a strip of fabric. Fold the sides to the middle, R/S out. Gather the layers using a hand running stitch. Sew in a diagonal manner across the strip. Use a strong thread. Pull up the thread to make the frill.

It is possible to do this on the machine and if so stitch the strip in short sections to reduce the stress on the thread when it is pulled up.

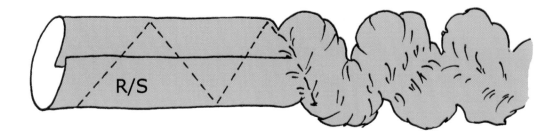

Ruched Box in Calico with tucked sides, free-motion quilted: Jennie Rayment

Weaving with Fabric

The traditional craft of weaving is an ancient art form, and has been part of the fundamental structure of our daily lives for thousands of years. All manner of fibres have been and are used to create a cloth of some description. There has been a vogue in recent times to resurrect ribbon weaving from the Victorian era.

During a flying visit to Los Angeles, I was ferreting round an interior design emporium and spotted a cushion that was made from woven and padded strips. It looked very similar to the method that I had been using to making bag handles. As a result, the aircraft could not fly back to England fast enough to let me get at the sewing machine and explore these ideas, and develop an easy way to incorporate 'Weaving with Bag Handles' into my work.

This is another textural creation that is really easy, and not only will you be able to weave with the strips, but the basic technique also makes exceedingly good handles! Take the opportunity to introduce some colour by experimenting with space-dyed or contrasting threads when you stitch the layers together, or change the backing material to a different shade. Consider varying the width, placement and colour of the woven bands to produce yet more exciting designs.

Remember that you can do anything you choose; it is not wrong, merely different! Once you understand the method, these ideas can be developed in a variety of ways.

Many different weaving designs can be translated in this fashion; look at books on ribbon weaving, study the structures of woven textiles and use the variety of woven formations to produce your own unique patterns using these padded strips.

Woven Cushions embellished with different stitches: Jennie Rayment

33

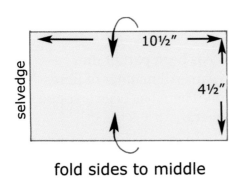

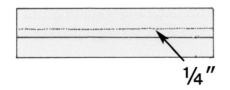

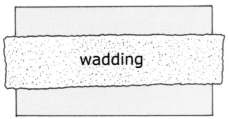

fold sides to middle

¼"

wadding

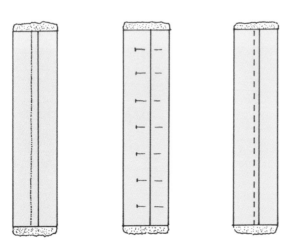

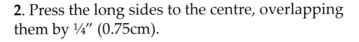

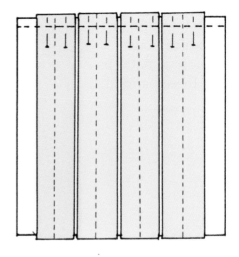

The measurements suggested in the following method will construct an 8" - 9" (20cm - 23cm) square approximately. You may choose to alter the sizes.

Preparing the Woven Strips

You need an 18" x 45" (20cm x 115cm) strip of fabric plus some small strips of 2 - 4oz wadding (batting).

1. From the fabric, cut eight strips of 4½" x 10" (11cm x 25cm). Do ensure that these are cut across the fabric from selvedge to selvedge.

2. Press the long sides to the centre, overlapping them by ¼" (0.75cm).

3. From the wadding, cut eight strips the length and width of the pressed strip. Open the strip and lay the wadding inside, as though you were wrapping a present.

4. Pin all the layers together, placing pins across the strip (baste the layers first if needed); then either by hand or machine, stitch down the centre of the strip; several rows of stitching may be done to create a quilted effect. Repeat with all eight strips.

5. Trim any surplus wadding away and check that all eight strips are the same length.

6. Cut a 10" (25cm) square from the calico, place four strips along one edge of the square, setting in ½" (1.25cm) from each side and positioning them evenly; pin well. Sew on the machine or hand-stitch firmly along the edge using a ½" (1.25cm) seam allowance.

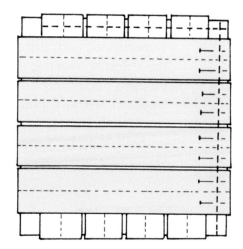

7. Repeat with the remaining four strips down the adjacent side, positioning equally as before, then sew firmly down the edge using ½"(1.25cm) seam allowance.

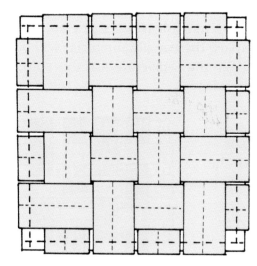

8. Weave together, under and over, as in a basic weaving design. Check the strips all lie parallel and are straight, before pinning firmly to the backing fabric, then sew down the remaining two sides, with the same seam allowance as before.

The panel is now ready to be framed with borders, and could be used for a cushion front, table mat, part of a textured wall-hanging, or set into another project such as a bag.

Woven Bag created from ten 4½" x 12" strips placed on a 12" square:
Jennie Rayment

Developing the Idea

Experiment with different widths of the padded strips, changing the colours, altering the weaving design, using a twin needle to create a decorative stitch down the padded bands, or explore the range of fancy stitches on the machine. It would be interesting to incorporate a variety of hand stitches - those who enjoy embellishing by hand could go to town with some fabulous stitch combinations!

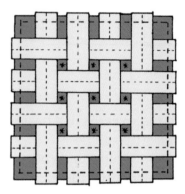

Change the backing square to a contrasting shade and space the strips further apart; the backing material will be revealed through the gaps in the weave. Repeat this colour in thread on the woven bands.

Explore the effect of two or more different colours for the strips.

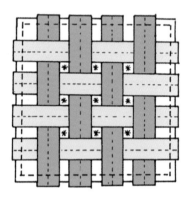

Play with weaving patterns, varying the width and the angle of the weaving.

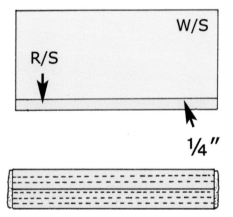

Use this technique to make comfortable and hard wearing bag handles:

Wrap up wadding in a long strip of material. Turn the raw edge under by ¼" (0.75cm) before pressing in place. Sew several lines of stitch to hold the layers together. (See page 107 for a simple bag pattern.)

36

Woven Handbag in calico: Jennie Rayment

'Quilt-as-you-go'

As the title indicates, your work can be given a quilted appearance by stitching the pieces together on a wadding (batting) backing. The stitching will not show as a surface decoration; it merely secures the fabric to the wadding.

I find that a layer of light-weight 'sew-in' interfacing underneath the fabric and above the wadding prevents the wadding from distorting and stretching as you sew the pieces in place. In addition lines can be drawn on the interfacing to indicate the placement of a specific section. This is very useful especially when making garments and will ensure the correct alignment of a textured section in the relevant position on the garment. The jacket featured in this book was constructed in this manner.

Using the 'Quilt-as-you-Go' method, Prairie Points, Somerset Patchwork, piping, frayed layers, extra wadding and many other insertions may be included within your design for an additional creative touch.

Crazy Patchwork from random strips, Log Cabin and Pineapple Patchwork can also be constructed with this method. The one drawback lies in the direction in which you stitch the pieces in place. 'Quilt-as-you-Go' has to be worked from the centre out or from an edge. It is possible to attach one of the strips incorrectly and have to cover the gap with a small amount of hand work or machine appliqué. Although, to be honest this may add a certain "je ne sais quoi" to the appearance, naturally you can say with great aplomb that the extra embellishment was by design!

The seam allowances can be your own personal choice. It is only necessary to use a ¼" (0.75cm) if you are trying to produce a panel of a specific size. It might be preferable to use an increased seam allowance to ensure that all the layers are enclosed by the seam. Unless you are working to a given size, minor deviations in the seam allowance do not matter; nor does it really affect the ultimate result, if the seam lines are not very straight. After all this is your own creation!

Parts of two waistcoats created with 'Quilt-as-you-Go' method: Jennie Rayment

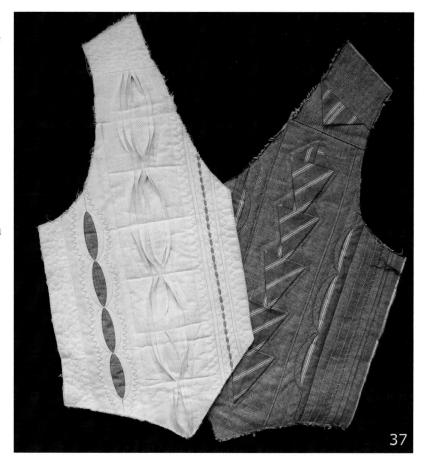

37

'Quilt-as-you-Go' Methods

Working from one Edge

1. Cut a piece of wadding and light-weight 'sew-in' interfacing large enough for the completed creation. (Iron-on interfacing is a total disaster as it can stick if you press the work.) Raid your stash for strips left over from other projects or cut up some scraps in different width strips.

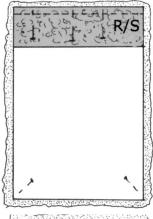

2. Lay the first piece of fabric R/S up along the top edge. Pin in place and stitch along the top edge to prevent it from moving. Sew close to the raw edge.

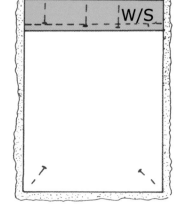

3. Lay the next strip W/S down, pin in place and stitch along the lower edge through all the layers.

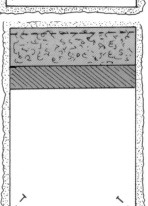

4. Open out and finger-press flat. Use the blunt end of your scissors or a ruler to help smooth the seam flat if necessary.

(Should you be using a cotton or wool based wadding it is possible to press the work, but don't iron when the wadding is a polyester or a polyester mixture as it can melt.)

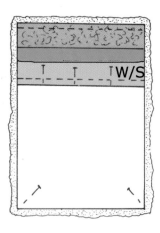
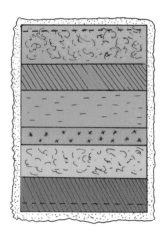

5. Add the next strip, remembering to lay it R/S down aligning the raw edge with the lower edge of the last piece. Pinning the layers each time helps to keep the strips flat. Sew along the lower edge through all the layers. Open out and finger press flat.

6. Continue in the same manner until the opposite side is reached; finally, stitch the outer edge of the last strip.

This 'Quilt-as-you-Go' sample can now be re-cut into any shape. Make it into a cushion, table-mat, hot water bottle cover or spectacle case. Lay a dressmaker's pattern on it and cut out clothing.

Adding Insertions to the Sample

Now you see how simple it is, try adding a few textural effects:

a. Once the first strip has been laid down, fold some squares into Prairie Points before you add the next piece.

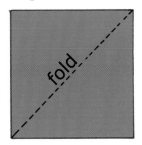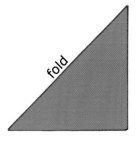

Cut a square of fabric (the size is irrelevant); fold once on the diagonal; fold again to form a triangle.

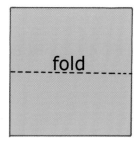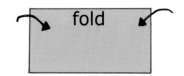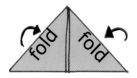

Alternatively insert some Somerset Patches:

Somerset Patches are squares folded in half across the centre then the corners on the folded edge are turned over to form a triangle. A Somerset Patch differs from a Prairie Point - there is a folded edge in the centre of the triangle unlike the other which has no centre fold.

Arrange these shapes along the raw edge of the last strip. They can be overlapped or spread out - the choice is yours. Check that all the raw edges are within the seam allowance.

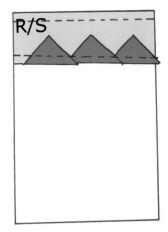

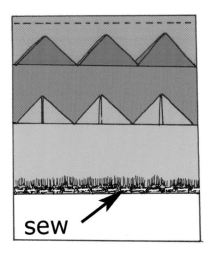

b. Insert some piping (page 98) between the strips for a little bit of textured embellishment.

c. Rip some fabric to make some frayed insertions (page 12). Tear thin strips, insert them in the seam, and then fray to the desired length. To make a thicker fringe, use several torn strips.

d. Ruche some fabric by gathering the opposite sides and insert into the work. Consider folding the ruched strip in half, stitch the sides together before inserting into the seam. (See page 29 for further ideas.)

e. Set a large zig-zag stitch on the machine, and meander at random over the fabric, altering the density of stitch as you sew. This creates a 'thread' textured material, which can be cut up and inserted into the work. Some of the space dyed/variegated machine threads look most attractive when used in this manner.

f. Why not include pieces of hand embroideries, odd remnants of textured sections, other types of fabric in the same colour tone, lace, ribbons and decorative braids? Nearly any scrap can be inserted into the work. You could even have a tassel!

It is preferable to stitch any textural supplement in place before the next layer is added to prevent it shifting. Use a long stitch length to secure the section in place. Sew within the seam allowance so that the stitching will not show when the next strip is attached. (It seems a waste of valuable time to do this anchoring, but the textured pieces seem to have a life of their own and a little demon moves them while you are not looking).

g. Include extra padding before attaching the next strip. Lift up the last piece, lay the padding under, pin the top fabric in place to prevent the padding escaping, stitch the edge of the top layer down before adding the next strip.

Keep going; you can add whatever relevant creations you desire.

Coloured fringing could be grass and a ruched section may be a rocky cluster. Adding some piping or some folded squares gives another textural dimension to the finished piece.

Textured Landscape created in the 'Quilt as you Go' method with the ruched forest appliquéed in place. Tucks, Zip Foot Tucks and ruched strips also included. For more precise information on constructing landscapes see Tucks & Textures Two: Jennie Rayment

Working from the Centre

'Quilt-as-you-Go' may be worked from the centre, from either a vertical, horizontal or diagonal strip or from a central shape.

Working with strips

Lay the centre section down first and pin in place. Attach another strip to either side. Continue in this fashion until the backing material is covered. Why not lay the strips at an angle, does everything always have to be in parallel lines? Remember to pin each additional strip in place and keep the work flat. On completion, trim the strips to align with the wadding and interfacing and stitch round the outer edges using a long stitch length to prevent the cut ends of the strips stretching.

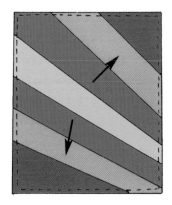

Working with a central shape

Place whatever shape you have chosen in the middle of the wadding. Sew in a clockwise or anti-clockwise pattern round a standard geometric form such as a square, remembering to open and flatten the layers as you go. Be systematic!

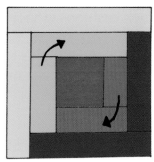

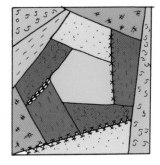

Should you select an abstract shape, take care to check that you cover all the raw edges when adding the next set of strips. Any small holes can be concealed with a little embroidery or a sneaky bit of hand stitching. This may even improve the whole appearance!

To sum up, this technique is both simple and effective; it is quick to produce and so useful to have at your fingertips. I could wax lyrical on the subject, so perhaps one day I will develop the theme.

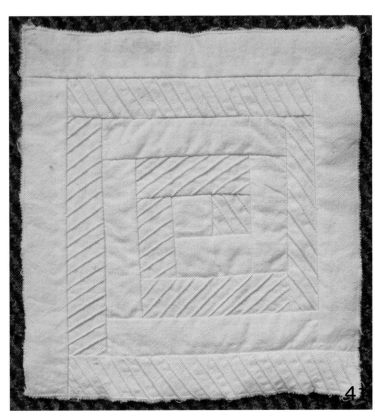

Spiral Log Cabin featuring strips cut from Pin tucked calico. Worked on polyester wadding using 'Quilt-as-you-Go' technique: Jennie Rayment

41

Delving into the Bias

When I first started investigating the potential of texturing surfaces, I played only with the straight grain of the material. But when I tried the bias grain, new horizons were opened.

Initially, I tried tucking down the bias without really thinking what would happen. As I flexed the tucks, they did not twist as before; they rolled back flat in an arc shape, just like the folds around the centre panel of Cathedral Window patchwork. It is amazing how blinkered one can be! If I had thought at all, the reason why the edges of Cathedral Windows roll is because they are on the bias grain.

From this beginning, a whole range of textural ideas has sprung. One of the cushions that is always popular features this effect; for some reason it appeals to everyone, particularly gentlemen. They appear to appreciate this textured design especially in calico. Having said that, the entire male population will now get bombarded with Bias Tuck cushions in various ways!

The potential of this technique is discussed at the end of the method - there are many possibilities for extending and interpreting the design.

There is only one rule to be followed:

Strips for Bias Tucks have to be cut on the bias.

42

Bias Tuck Cushion made from bias strips arranged on calico. Machine quilted: Jenne Rayment

Preparing the Bias Strips

To make a 18" (45cm) cushion front you need a 36" x 40/45" (100cm x 115cm) strip of fabric plus an 18" x 32" (50cm x 90cm) piece of 2oz. wadding (batting).

1. Cut a 15" x 40/45" (38cm x 90cm) strip from the fabric (it's much easier to cut bias strips from a smaller piece of material and creates less waste).

2. Use the rotary cutter and ruler to cut the bias strips. Position the ruler so the 45° line aligns with the selvedge. If your ruler lacks this line try using the drawn lines on the cutting mat, lay the fabric out flat and align the ruler with the 45° line imprinted on the board.

(These photographs are for cutting bias strips with the right-hand. Left-handed people hold the photograph up to a mirror.)

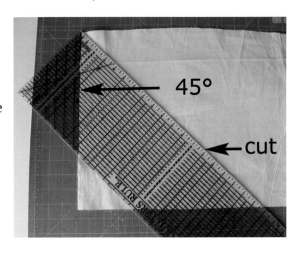

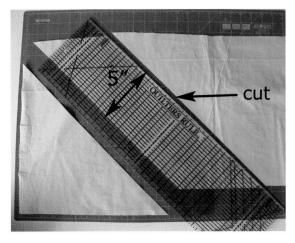

3. Make the first cut across the fabric. Measure 5" (12 cm) from the diagonally cut edge and cut another strip. Keep cutting until you have five to six pieces.

4. Cut a 15" (38cm) square for backing the design from the remaining fabric. Also cut a square of 2oz. wadding (batting) slightly larger than this. Pin the four corners of the backing square to the wadding.

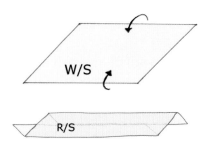

5. Press the bias strips - long sides to middle (just touching), this resembles giant bias binding.

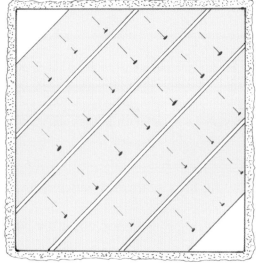

Cover the backing square with these pressed bands. Make sure that the raw edge on the back of the pressed band is underneath. Trim the excess fabric to match the backing square.

Remove the first four pins once the pressed bands have been pinned in place.

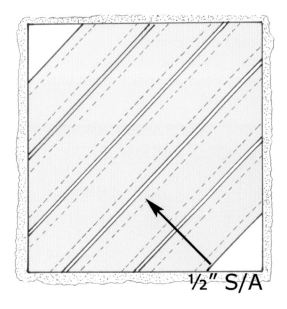

6. Using ½″ (1.25cm) S/A, sew up and down all the edges of the bias strips. Lengthen the stitch length on the machine to 3mm as sewing through thick layers of wadding and fabric will contract the stitch length. If sewing by hand, use a small firm back stitch.

To achieve an accurate ½″ (1.25cm) seam, mark the seam: Rule a line at this distance or score the fabric - run the point of a stitch ripper, blunt screwdriver, barbecue skewer or similar down the edge of the ruler. (There is a gadget available for scoring fabric but these other devices can be substituted.) Alternatively, move the needle to the left-hand side of the presser foot - on some models the needle can be set exactly ½″ (1.25cm)) from the presser foot edge.

½″ S/A

7. Open the Bias tucks and embellish the channel with a decorative machine stitch, hand embroidery, ribbon or lace. (Lay thin paper under the backing material to prevent the fabric distorting when sewing any heavy satin stitch design.) This decoration will be revealed when the pleats are rolled back.

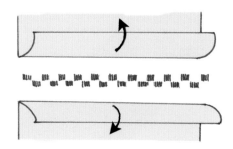

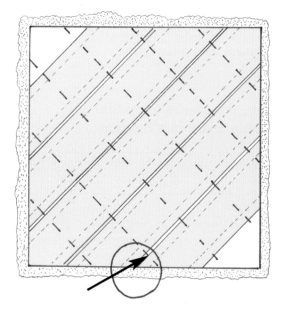

8. Close the tucks again; carefully mark equal divisions, approximately 2½″ (6.5cm) apart across the square on the opposing diagonal; use a hard (H) pencil or a washable/vanishing ink pen.

Check that the ink will vanish or wash out. Sometimes the marks return, especially if you have pre-washed the fabric, as the residue of the detergent can chemically affect the ink thus rendering it visible again. Not a happy situation!

Ensure that these lines cross the sewn ones, allowing for a seam allowance round the outside of the panel.

9. Sew along these lines, either by hand or machine.

10. Roll back the edges of the Bias Tucks - these tucks will roll backwards in an arc shape as in Cathedral Window patchwork. Pin the tucks flat.

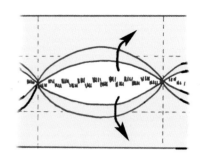

11. Sew along the outer edge of rolled back tuck; use a blind hem, small appliqué, fine satin stitch, or any hand stitch. Consider the effect of a contrasting coloured thread for added oomph!

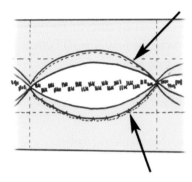

Invisible thread will conceal a multitude of mistakes. Remember to have cotton thread on the bottom bobbin.

The settings for a very fine blind hem stitch on many machines are:
1 - stitch length, 1 - stitch width.
Use the normal straight stitch presser foot or an open toe (Bernina users - re-align the needle position to the centre).

Roll back the tucks between the lines of stitch to form a 'bobble' or oval shape, the embroidery will show in the open space. Leave the tucks along the outer edges flat (unrolled) and stitch in place.

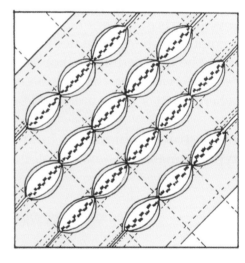

12. Trim off any uneven edges, and square up the design.

13. Add a 2½" (6.5cm) border to all sides. Place the bordered panel onto another square of wadding. Pin the four corners before adding a few lines of straight or decorative stitch on the border around the central panel.

Calico Bias Tuck Cushion:
Jennie Rayment

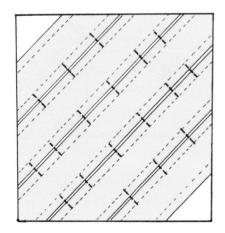

Further Experiments with the Bias

a. Change the size of the 'bobbles' by altering the distance between the diagonal lines of stitching - choose to have 'bobbles' in different sizes. (Less than 1½" (4cm) in length is difficult to roll back.) By anchoring the tucks down in an uneven format, you can mix the sizes of the ovals.

b. Try catching the rolled edges down in one or two places only, or at the mid-point with a few small hand stitches or perhaps a French Knot or two.

c. Roll open only one side of the tuck or part of one as shown below.

d. Consider arranging the bias strips vertically or horizontally on the backing fabric.

e. The backing material could be a patterned cloth, arrange the 'bobbles' to roll back and reveal parts of the print. Striped designs may be used to good effect. Some fabrics have a colour wash in graduated tones and different shades, an interesting array of colours could be revealed in the 'bobbles'. Alternatively, lay a strip of contrasting coloured fabric between the channels before sewing across the bias strips, the colour will appear when the Bias Tucks are rolled back.

f. Construct the bias strips from chintz, lay them on to silk. Experiment with different types of materials. Imagine all the possibilities!

Play on!

Bias Tuck in a Square

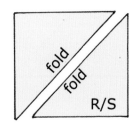 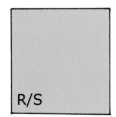

1. Cut three squares same size. Fold two squares in half diagonally; lay them on to the third square R/S up and pin in place.

2. Stitch ½″ (1.25cm) seam down either side of the centre folds to make the tucks. Open the channel between the tucks and embellish. Anchor the tuck edges a short distance from the corner of the square.

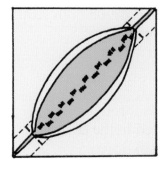

3. Roll back the tucks in the centre and stitch in place.

This square could be inserted into a corner on a quilt, used in a pelmet or any border design. Four panels would make a cushion cover.

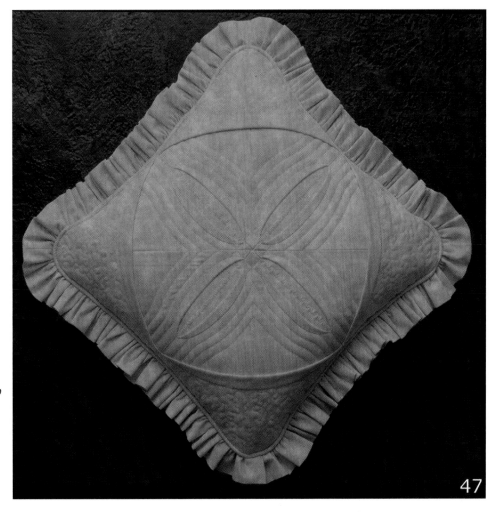

Four Bias Tuck in a Square sewn together. To make the arced border, fold four extra squares diagonally into triangles and apply one to each corner. Roll back the folded edge of these triangles and sew in place: Jennie Rayment

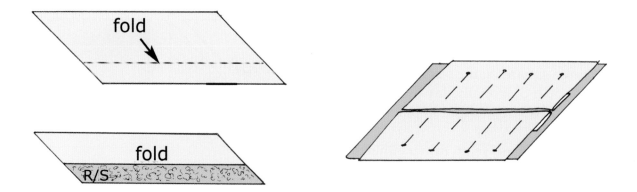

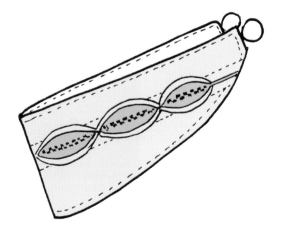

Inserting a Single Bias Tuck Band

1. Cut two bias strips. Press 1" (2.5cm) to W/S along one long edge. Position both strips on an additional straight cut strip, butting the folds in the centre, pin well.

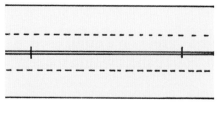

2. Stitch ½" (1.25cm) from the folds through all the layers. Embroidery may be included in the channel. Secure the folds. Roll back and catch down.

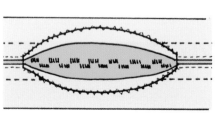

Insert this strip into a tie-back, waistband, waistcoat, belt or a jacket sleeve - it is not dissimilar to the Elizabethan slashed sleeves.

It looks good, it's easy and it's different!

Bias Waistband on circular skirt: Jennie Rayment

Trumpets

The idea for this design came like a bolt from the blue, it was definitely one of my better moments for thinking up new techniques. This was going to be yet another day when the housework went to pot; I had to play! Since teaching patchwork, I have discovered all kinds of sneaky tricks to convince the nearest and dearest that I have been hard at work 'doing' the housework. There is nothing like a few track lines from the Hoover on the carpet; pictures knocked slightly askew and merrily boiling saucepans containing only water and a stock cube to preserve the illusion that one has been frantically busy all day. The microwave rules OK!

Finally, after many experiments, lots of stitched and semi-sewn blocks, a wastepaper bin full of scraps, I had a viable design that I could teach. What was I going to call my novel construction?

Trumpets was the final choice and is infinitely preferable to 'Squashed Prairie Points' although this is what they are! The name arose from the somewhat vague appearance of the shape to a trumpet. "Of course", I hear you say!

Silk Trumpets with ruched piping:
Jennie Rayment

49

Composing the Trumpet

The seam allowance for this design is ³/₈″ (1cm) **NOT ¼″ (0.75cm)**. The reason for this sized seam allowance is to ensure that all the layers of fabric are caught in the seam, if too narrow a seam is used then there is a possibility that one of the layers may slip out of the seam.

1. Cut eight equal sized squares from a light or medium weight fabric; these can any dimension - 6″ (15cm) is a good starting point. Use the rotary cutter and ruler to cut a 6″ (15cm) strip from the material; subdivide this strip into the squares.

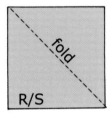
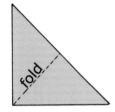
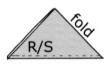

2. Fold four of the squares into triangles, press gently; using a long stitch length or small tacking stitch, baste the raw edges together. Sew within the ³/₈″ (1cm) S/A.

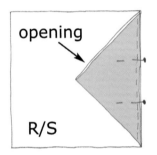
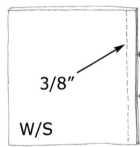

3. Lay one of these triangles on the R/S of one of the other squares, aligning all the raw edges. Pin in place. Lay another square on top (forming a sandwich); stitch the layers together with ³/₈″ (1cm) seam.

4. Press the seam open and flat.

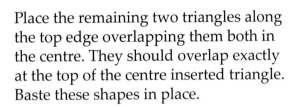

5. Repeat this operation with the remaining two squares and one more triangle.

6. Open one of the sets of stitched squares. Lay it down with the inserted triangle opening facing the top.

Place the remaining two triangles along the top edge overlapping them both in the centre. They should overlap exactly at the top of the centre inserted triangle. Baste these shapes in place.

Check the opening of each inserted triangle faces the centre of the design, it is easy to make a mistake!

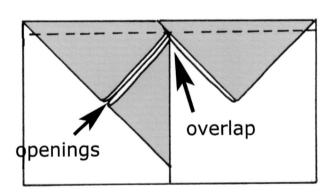

6. Open the remaining section (with the triangle insert) and lay it on top. Turn this inserted triangle so that the two centre triangles lie back to back. Check that the opening of the triangle faces the middle of the block.

7. Pin the layers together and sew along the edge. Change the machine needle to 90 - 100 (14 - 16) as there are so many layers.

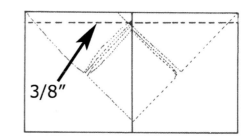

3/8"

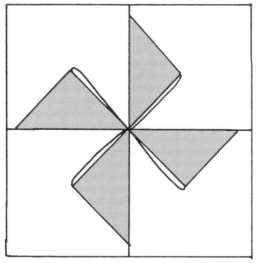

Open out and lay the block flat. Amazingly there are four triangles inserted between four squares.

Due to the thickness of the fabrics, the centre junction of all the triangle tips may not be quite accurate. A covered button or attractive bead conceals any misdemeanour!

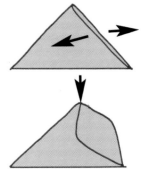

8. Lift the one of the triangles. Pull the sides apart and flatten the triangle downwards to form a kite shape. Repeat with the other three triangles and there they are... Four Trumpets.

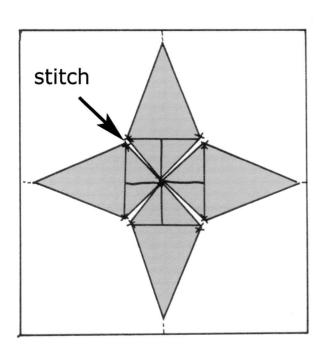

stitch

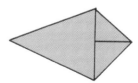

9. Catch the corners of each Trumpet with a small stitch to hold the shape flat.

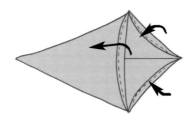

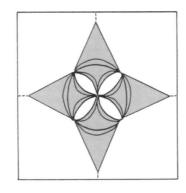

10. Roll back the edges of the Trumpets and stitch the folds down through all the layers. (See page 45 for some advice on stitching techniques.)

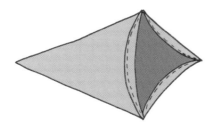

There are many different ideas you can now explore:

a. Cover the seam line in the centre of the Trumpet with a triangular scrap of fabric. What about a contrasting colour? Roll the edges of the Trumpet to cover the raw sides of this additional scrap.

b. Insert a Somerset Patch (page 38).

c. Stuff the Trumpets with a small quantity of wadding, or even some pot pourri; then sew the open edge down to hold the filling in place.

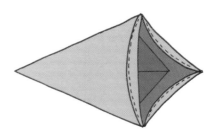

d. Do all three ideas for a really effective piece of textural work.

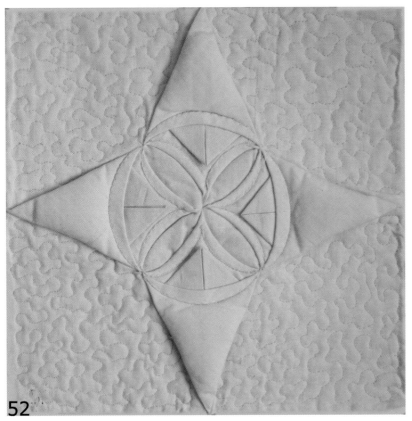

You may wish to quilt this design. Sometimes it is easier to quilt the block before stitching the corners of the Trumpets in place. Complete the quilting, then open and flatten the Trumpets and secure the corners in place.
(For quilting hints see pages 94 - 97.)

Trumpet Block with Somerset Patches: Jennie Rayment

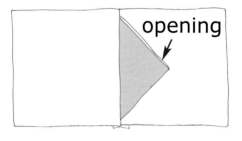

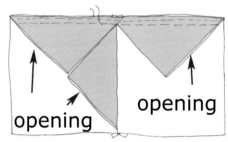

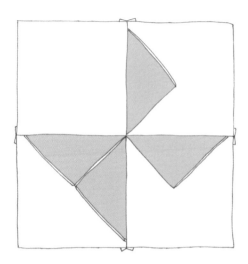

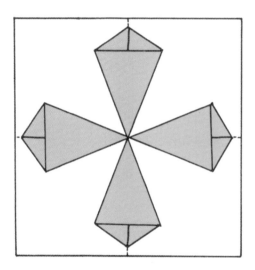

Something different!

Arrange the Trumpets the other way round with all the openings away from the centre.

1. Follow Stages 1 - 8 (pages 50 - 51) BUT this time turn each Trumpet round so that the opening is away from the centre of the block - facing the outside edge.

2. Open out the shapes and secure on the corners with a few stitches.

This makes a cross that is not dissimilar to the Viking sign of blessing on rune stones.

Yet again, the Trumpets can be padded, rolled and have various insertions.

Why not play with the shapes and see what happens?

Four ways to play with Trumpets: Jennie Rayment

53

For a different arrangement, cut a large square into four triangles and put a Trumpet in the seams. ?

Don't forget that buttons are brill in the centre if the points don't line up!

Additional ideas with a Trumpet

There is no reason why Trumpets can't be inserted into any seam. Sandwiching one between two triangles, then the Trumpet will be on the diagonal.

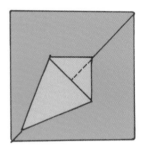

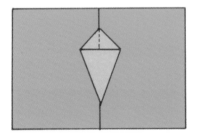

Trumpets can be made from any size of square. Try a small one inserted between two large squares; it can be positioned at any distance from the top of the square and which-ever way round you choose.

Introduce one into a table-mat for holding a napkin. Use several as pockets for an Advent Calendar. Large Trumpets could be part of a shoe tidy, or a child's wall-hanging to hold little toys.

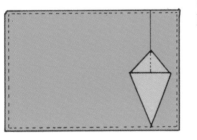

Small Trumpets could be a decorative feature on the shoulders of fashion garments.

Explore the effectiveness of this shape as florets, similar to Bluebells or Delphiniums. (Stretching a point I know, but why not?)

The Triangle Cornet

A rare musical instrument! It is a cousin of the Trumpet as it can also be inserted into any seam, manipulated in many ways and constructed from any size of triangle. It is not complicated to create as all you do is cut a square in half. Simple!

 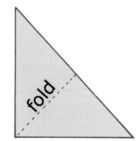

1. Cut a 6″ (15cm) square in half on the diagonal forming two triangles.

2. Take one of the triangles and fold R/S together. Stitch along the bias side of the triangle (stretchy side). Be careful not to distort the bias edge as you sew. Use a narrow seam allowance.

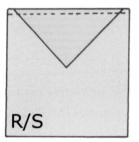 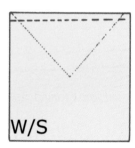

3. Clip the point off the end of the seam before turning the triangle R/S out.

4. Cut two more 6″ (15cm) squares. Lay the triangle on one 6″ (15cm) square. Pin in place. Lay the other 6″ (15cm) square on top R/S down aligning the raw edges (follow the Trumpet technique page 50). Stitch the seam using ³/₈″ (1cm) S/A.

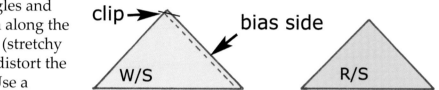

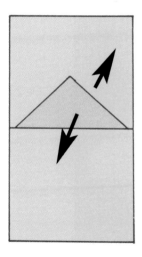 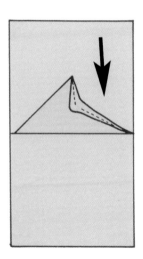 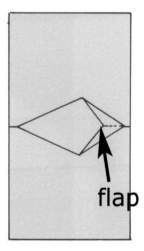

5. Press the seam open and flat. Lift the triangle and pull the sides apart. Flatten it down to form a kite shape but unlike the Trumpet, there is a little flap - more possibilities for play!

Developing the Design

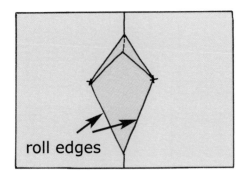

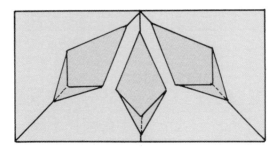

a. Secure the corners of the shape to the base material then roll the edges inwards.

The flap can be turned in either direction and stitched in place. Addition of a bead or French Knots on the stitching may add a little extra decoration.

b. Insert the Triangle Cornet between triangles. Eight T/Cs make a Star Design as shown below.

c. Explore the possibilities of this textural insert by sandwiching it between triangles or placing several in a line down the sleeve of a garment.

d. Why not experiment with the Triangle Cornets by reversing every other one, alternate with Trumpets in a seam or as a block design?

"In creating, the only hard thing's to begin;
A grass blade's no easier to make than an oak."
James Russell Lowell 1848

And you are only making a Triangle Cornet!

Don't forget that buttons and beads are most excellent for embellishing and use of them in judicious places can conceal all manner of misdemeanours!

Eight Triangle Cornets set close to the centre. TCs inserted between eight triangles. Completed with ruched piping: Jennie Rayment

The Trumpet Voluntary!

As you will discover when you start to play with folded shapes, there are many other variations on a theme. This one is formed from a Prairie Point (page 38).

1. Construct a Prairie Point. Fold **A** (tip of the triangle) back to touch **C**. Repeat with the other tip of the triangle **B**. Baste the layers together along the raw edges to prevent any movement of the folds.

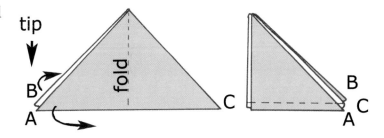

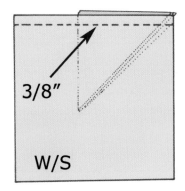

2. Sandwich this shape between two squares or triangles. Pin the layers together and stitch with $^3/_8$″ (1cm) S/A.

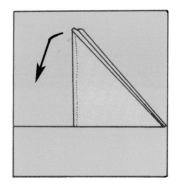

3. Pull the shape backwards to touch the base material. Open the folds and flatten. It might require a modicum of tweaking to get the shape to lie evenly. The final shape will have a kite-like appearance.

Catch the corners on to the base material with a stitch. Beads would be an excellent embellishment. Why not play with rolling the folds back or place some padding underneath before stitching the shape in place?

Experiment with inserting this shape between six 60° triangles for an interesting box lid (photograph page 60).

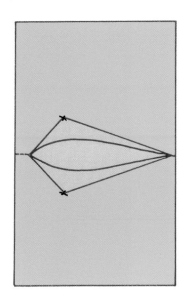

Hat Box, Lifted Star Cushion & Napkins. Hat Box displays six Trumpet Voluntary shapes and has Bow Tie panels with pin tucked inserts. Napkins feature frayed edges and the napkin rings are created from padded bands:
Jennie Rayment

Trumpet Voluntary cushion with Origami Twists:
Shelagh Jarvis

Lifted Star

The Lifted Star patchwork (sometimes called the Raised Star) has been included in this book as it looks very ornamental in one colour, most attractive in several colours, and is easy to make; the main drawback lies in the fact that it uses a vast amount of fabric. Another problem is washing the completed Star. Dry cleaning may be the answer as it is such a dense design and it will take a long time to dry unless tumbled; but for a rapid textural effect that appears highly impressive, it is hard to beat. This is also ideal for a gift and will delight the recipient, who will be amazed at your professional skill

Although actual design of this patchwork greatly resembles Somerset or Folded Patchwork, the construction is completely different. It is preferable to use the sewing machine because there are many layers which make the design difficult to hand sew. (Somerset Patchwork can be done more easily by hand.)

As the Lifted Star is composed on eight lines, the final structure is octagonal, as opposed to Somerset Patchwork which can be created in a circle. In addition, this patchwork has the same number of sections on each of the 45° lines, unlike the former which has more pieces added at other degree measurements as the design expands.

As there are a large amount of squares to be cut; it is advantageous to use a rotary cutter, mat and ruler. Also these squares have to be pressed beforehand so the preparation work can be time-consuming, once that's done the design will grow quickly.

Lifted Star Cushions in chintz and calico: Jennie Rayment

The basic measurements are given below; further ideas for selecting colours and design development are included at the end of the method.

To make a 11″ (28cm) - 12″ (30cm) Lifted Star

You need approximately 1 yard (1 metre) of cotton/silk/chintz or any other medium weight material plus extra material for the borders. In addition, you need one 14″ - 15″ (35cm - 38cm) square of firmly woven medium-weight backing fabric. Light-weight finely woven materials will not support the weight of the Lifted Star and will distort in the construction process.

1. Cut forty-eight 6″ (15cm) squares from the fabric. These could all be the same colour or cut twenty-four of each.

To make the cutting easier: Iron the fabric beforehand, fold into four, lining up the selvedges with the central fold. Cut a 6″ (15cm) strip from the material using the rotary cutter. Re-cut the strip vertically into 6″ squares.

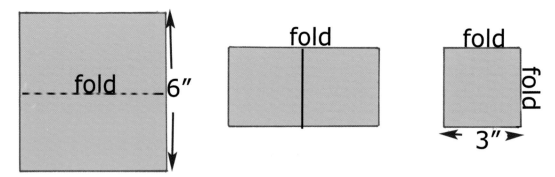

Fold each square in half along the straight grain of the fabric (into a rectangle) and press. Fold again to form a smaller square, repeat the pressing forming forty-eight 3″ (7.5cm) squares.

Alternative method for preparing the forty-eight 'squares' - saves some material!

As you will discover, the Lifted Star eats fabric; there is an alternative method of cutting out the squares. Cut a 6″ (15cm) strip; cut off as many 6″ (15cm) squares as possible, stop when the remainder of the strip measures less than 12″ (30cm); divide this in half. The pieces must measure 6″ (15cm) in one direction. These odd-sized scraps are folded with the shorter edge on the right-side, and then pressed so they measure 3″ (7.5cm) square, with the shorter length on the outside.

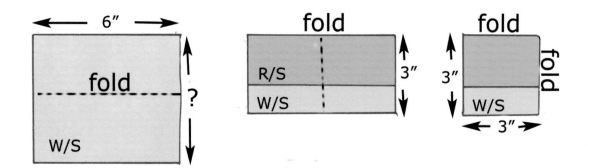

2. Fold the 14″ - 15″ (35cm -38cm) square in half from side to side and then in half again to find the centre. Press well.

3. On the pressed square, draw the eight major lines of the compass, extending the lines across the whole of the backing piece. This can be done by folding the material again and pressing the creases including those on the diagonal, but it is more accurate to use a protractor and mark equal divisions of 45°.

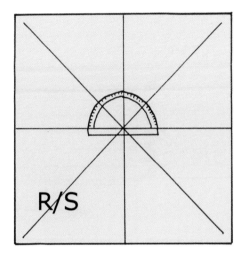

Place the protractor on the centre of the square, lining the little cross on the middle of the protractor with the centre. Now mark off the 0°, 45°, 90°, 135°, 180° points, turn the protractor round and mark the 45°, 90°, 135° points. Join all the lines through the centre mark, extending across the entire fabric. The lines need to be long.

4. Complete the preparations by cutting a small 1″ (2.5cm) square off the corner of one of the cut squares or from a scrap of spare material.

Method for Sewing the Star.

1. Place the 1″ (2.5cm) square in the centre of the drawn lines; this prevents the lines showing through any gap in the pieces. Divide the forty-eight squares into eight sets of six squares, one set for every line.

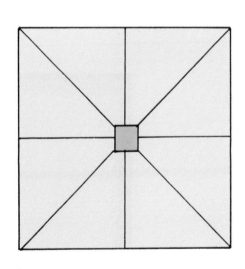

2. Select one of the lines, open out one of the squares to form a rectangle, and line up the pressed crease with the drawn line, positioning the fold of the rectangle $\frac{1}{16}$″ (0.2cm) or thereabouts i.e. a fraction away from the centre.

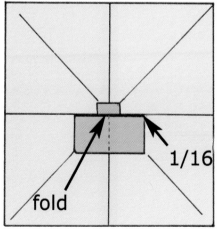

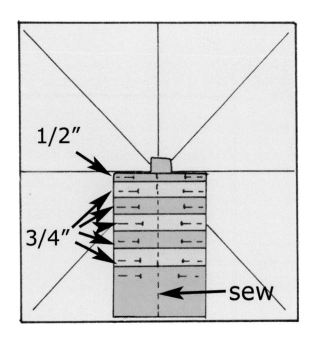

3. Open the remaining five pressed squares to form rectangles and place along the same line. Space them apart using the measurements shown in the diagram. Pin all the sections firmly through to the backing fabric.

By replacing the pins with Sellotape, or similar type of sticky tape, the sections can be secured to the backing material; this saves time and is just as accurate. (See the photograph below.)

4. Following the creased line, stitch outwards from the centre; sew to the end of all the folded sections.

5. Repeat this operation on all the remaining lines, using the same accurate spacing of each of the six sections.

Check that the edges of any previously attached sections are not caught in the next line of stitching - push all the pieces out of the way as you attach each line.

6. Begin to fold:

Open out two of the stitched lines of six sections to reveal the backing fabric.

Take the top left-hand piece and fold in half diagonally forming a triangle. The fabric is folded to the underside.

Lay this triangle on to the backing fabric. Take the top right-hand side, fold in half diagonally.

Lay the right-hand triangle on top of the left-hand one.

Take the second left-hand section, fold diagonally, and place on top. Repeat with the right-hand side etc. Keep folding in the same manner until you reach the last section. Take care to fold each piece carefully keeping the diagonal fold bisecting the corner.

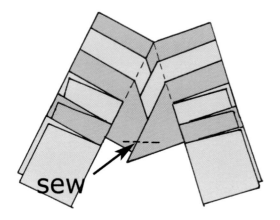

It is advisable, after folding the third set into triangles, to sew through all the layers and secure the pieces firmly to the backing fabric.

Failing to do this may mean that your work gets destroyed when impish fingers pull the folds out!

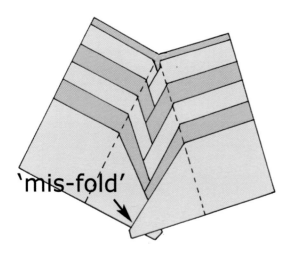

7. Fold the last set obliquely - not on the true diagonal i.e. 'mis-fold'. If this last set is not 'mis-folded', the Lifted Star will not lie flat.

Be careful to ensure that both sides overlap.

Repeat the folding on every line. Check that the tips of the Star sections are all equal measurements from the centre point, otherwise the octagonal effect will be lost when the border is added.

8. Now the folding is complete, rule a line around the Star.

Place the rotary rule, so the ¼" (or metric equivalent) line passes through the tips of the Star, and draw a line from tip to tip. This line will be useful as an accurate positioning line for adding the triangles to convert the octagon into a square.

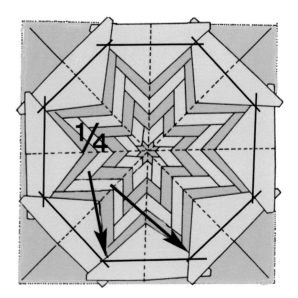

9. Sew round the edge of the Star on this ruled line to hold all the folded layers in place.

10. Cut two extra 6″(15cm) squares, divide on the diagonal forming four triangles. Place these so the longest side (bias) of the triangle is aligned exactly with the drawn and stitched line. Pin and stitch along the edge, using a ¼″(0.75cm) S/A. Stitch all four triangles in place. Open out and press.

(These triangles are technically too large and may overhang the seam, this may be useful when squaring up the block. More is <u>sometimes</u> better than less except when it is something nice, then more is <u>always</u> better!

11. Trim off any excess fabric and 'square up' the design. Press gently.

Add borders for a cushion, bind for a pleasing table-mat or box lid. The completed design is very heavy, it might not be very suitable for a quilt block.

Any small gaps in the centre of the Star can be covered with an attractive button, bead, some embroidery, or even a small tassel if the Lifted Star is to be used as a lid.

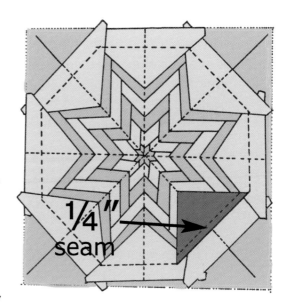

Extensions to Design

1. Explore the use of colour in the Star by choosing a greater selection of colours. Consider the effect of tones of the same hue ranging from light to dark.

Fascinating spiral patterns could be constructed by arranging the colours sequence carefully.

Think about changing the colour sequence in alternate rows, then change the folding pattern. Instead of folding right over left consistently, change to alternating the folding i.e. right over left then left over right etc. This will have the effect of making some colours seem more dominant than others. Look at the picture on the opposite page.

2. How about changing the size of the basic squares and making the Lifted Star bigger or smaller?

a. Cut 3″ (7.5cm) squares and halve all the spacing measurements. Leave the $\frac{1}{16}$″ (0.2cm) measurement as it is at the centre, but divide all the other measurements in half; $\frac{1}{4}$″, $\frac{3}{8}$″, $\frac{3}{8}$″ etc. (0.75cm, 1cm, 1cm).

b. Cut 4″ (10cm) basic squares, then divide all the measurements pro rata (i.e. two-thirds of the original set spacings).

c. The Star can be increased by adding larger squares to the same lines, but this becomes very heavy. It would need a larger piece of backing fabric to mount the design on.

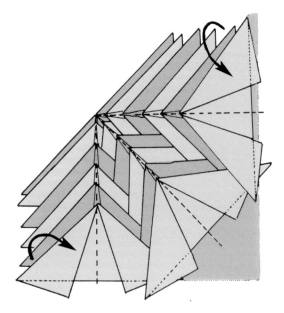

d. Change the folding design by folding the sections forwards. When the last set is mis-folded, a gap will appear forming a further textural effect.

This could be enhanced by constructing the last sets of squares from different coloured rectangles.

Sew two 3½″ x 6″ (8cm x 15cm) rectangles together. Press the seam and fold in half along the seam line.

3. For an unusual design, divide the backing square into equal divisions of 30°. Place the protractor in the centre and mark out at 30° intervals. Rule through all the degree markings to form twelve lines.

Cut four 6″ (15cm) squares for each line and fold in half. Lay four on each of the twelve lines. The spacing between the sections has to be adjusted. Lay the first section $^1/_{16}$″ away from the centre (described on page 61). Alter the other measurements to 1½″; 1¼″; 1¼″ (4cm, 3cm, 3cm).

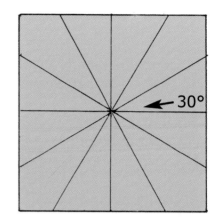

4. Insert a quarter of the Star on a corner of a border, creating an intriguing textural dimension to your quilt or wall-hanging.

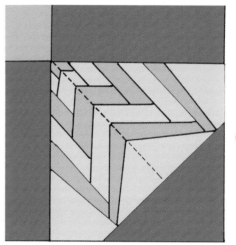

This design makes wonderful cushions. In the smaller size it is very good for a hat box lid, needlework case or basket. Made up in Christmas fabrics, it will be a stunning wall-hanging.

Lifted Star - twelve divisions. Alternating the folding of the squares on every other section:
Jennie Rayment

From Knits to Knots

Did you think that this book was about sewing? It is but there are times when knitting and knotting will give just that little added extra oomph!

Knitted material has a splendid texture, and can be used in the centre of Cathedral Window patchwork, the Origami Twist or Bow Tie. It can be inserted into cushions, bags, incorporated as panels in clothing or even used to make rugs and table-mats.

No one thought you were eccentric until now. But when your husband arrives home and discovers you solemnly cutting a square of fabric into a long strip, then winding it into a ball and knitting with it, he will think that you have reached the point of no return. It may possibly cross his mind that you have squandered the housekeeping and cannot afford any knitting wool, so had to resort to an alternative.

Just accept the fact that you are , like all of us, charmingly potty; but here is a way to use up all the old scraps that have been hoarded for years. 1960's crimplene, lengths of furnishing fabrics, chintzes, those vibrantly coloured pieces that were "a good idea at the time" - in fact any fabric will knit. You could convert all those polythene carrier bags into a knitted section for a fully washable, wipe-able and hard-wearing mat.

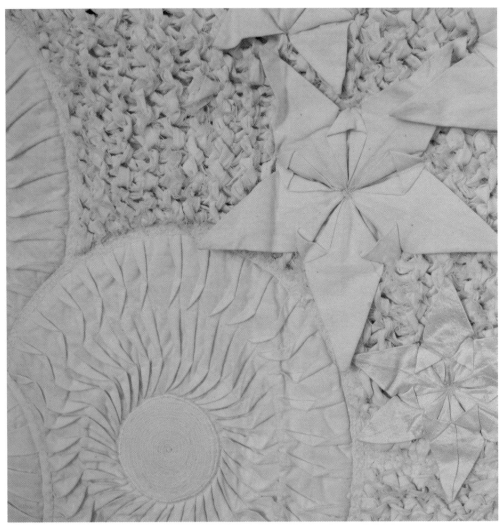

Knitted calico with appliquéed Tucked Circles and 3D stars: Jennie Rayment

Knitting Technique

Cut large rectangles or squares from the material, round off the corners, then starting at one edge, cut a ½″ (1.25cm) strip, round and round the shape. Keep going until the centre is reached, wind into a ball and begin to knit.

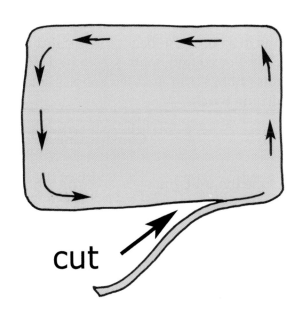

cut

Beware: The piece of fabric will reduce to approximately one-eighth of its area when knitted up.

Select large wooden, plastic or steel needles. Cast on loose stitches, and keep the tension fairly slack; fabric lacks the same elasticity as wool with the exception of stretch materials e.g. crimplene. If the strip breaks, either weave in the next length or knot the broken ends together.

Basic garter stitch (plain knitting) is a good choice and produces a pleasing knobbly texture, although you could experiment with other knitting designs.

When you have knitted sufficient for the desired space, straighten the section and reinforce the outer edge by stitching round on the sewing machine. This prevents it all from unravelling should any trimming be required.

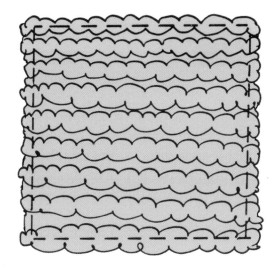

Do not disregard that unattractive patterned material with big splodges of colour, it will change its appearance remarkably when knitted. The patterns break up and the colours diffuse into a pleasing haze of tints, tones and shades. Glazed cotton (chintz) knits well and the sheen catches the light as the strips twist in and out in the knitting structure.

As suggested at the beginning, there are many places where knitted fabrics can be used so gather up all those ancient materials, cut into them into strips and start knitting.

Create a textural and tactile panel for a cushion. Knit blocks for a cot quilt or small mat. If you kept going you could knit a new rug for the sitting room, plastic bags would be an excellent choice - the rug would be washable and wear well unless you select those biodegradable ones that seem to degrade as you walk out of the shop! Get the children in on the act, knitting is not difficult and if they are not old enough to knit them they can wind the strips into balls. Dream on!

Plaiting and Knotting

Add other textured effects to your creations by plaiting strips together or by tying a few knots in a band. Tie-backs for curtains can be made from plaited strips, using the curtain material or complimentary coloured cloth. Make comfortable and strong handles for all kinds of bags from padded bands plaited together. Add a knotted band for that unusual finishing touch.

Constructing a Plait

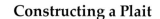

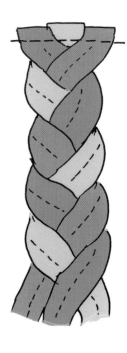

The width of the finished plait will depend on the intended use. Tie-backs need fairly wide, well-padded bands, the dimensions of plaits for handles and straps will be in proportion to the bag size.

1. Make 3 long padded strips (page 34). As a guide to estimating the approximate length required for your chosen project, plaiting contracts the length by approximately two-thirds.

2. Lay the strips together, the outer two set fractionally over the centre one; stitch to secure.

3. Plait the strips - right over centre, left over centre etc. Place the sewing foot presser foot on the start to anchor the bands while you plait.

4. Stitch the ends together before inserting.

There is no reason why ribbons or threads cannot be incorporated into the piece, or why the strips have to be the same dimension - mix thick and thin strips in a plaited formation. Investigate other types of plait - try different plaiting weaves with more strips.

Plaits could be used as a decorative edge for a cushion. Attach plaited piping cords and braids to pelmets echoing the textured tie-backs. How about a central panel for a cushion - weave plaits in and out? Create a matching hair band or belt as a fashionable accessory. Why not!

As an alternative to plaiting fabric, tie knots. Knotted strips can be employed in a similar way. Short lengths with either one or two knots could be incorporated in your work; the knots could be arranged in a sequence or an abstract pattern. Experiment with different types of knots, or possibly tie several knots together.

A panel of knotted strips could be embellished with bead work, or embroidered as further ornamentation.

70

Frayed Fabrics

Rip the cloth for an interesting frayed textural insert (see page 38) or fringe the fibres for a decorative finishing touch.

Create some attractive table linen by fringing the edges of tablecloths and napkins:

Tear the material to the desired size. Select a decorative stitch, possibly one of the stretch stitches like the honeycomb (if your machine does not have any fancy stitches, use two narrow rows of fine straight stitches instead). Sew round the article keeping the presser foot approximately ½" (1.25cm) from the edge of the fabric. Fray the threads by pulling the long fibres out. Stop the fraying two or three fibres from the stitching line.

If you choose to use one of the heavier embroidery stitches, placing paper underneath the material will prevent any buckling of the cloth. The paper will tear away easily afterwards, leaving a residue under the threads which will soften with wear and washing.

Knotted padded strips form the front panel of this simple bag. Handles constructed from knitted padded bands:
Jennie Rayment

71

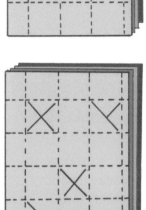

Slashed Fabric

There are several textile artists who specialise in this technique and produce some amazing textural effects. Whether you work with different colours or just choose one, once slashed and washed, the result is interesting.

One method to make a slashed section is to stitch a pad of fabrics together. Prepare a pad composed of four or five layers of material. Use a fairly firm material as a base with lighter weight fabrics on top. You may choose to have the darkest colour on the top with the brighter hues underneath. These will be revealed when the material is slashed.

Sew straight lines of stitching through all the layers in a square grid format.

Once the pad has been stitched, the layers of fabric should be cut on the bias/diagonal (this is necessary or the material will fray away completely). Snip through some or all of the layers, cutting on the diagonal. It is unnecessary to slash along every diagonal, leave some parts of the grid intact.

The pad is then washed, and placed in the tumble dryer. This causes the cut sections to roll outwards for maximum textural effect.

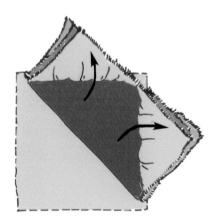

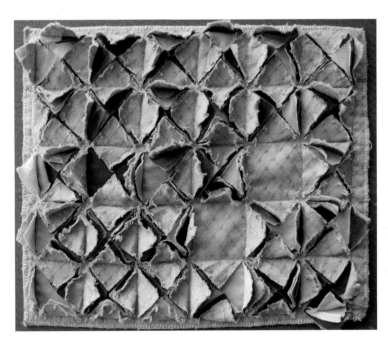

To sum up this chapter...

For that little additional extra touch - you could knit, plait, slash or even fray it!!

Why Knot!

Origami Twist

Origami is the art of folding paper and it is uncertain whether it originated from the Japanese, Koreans or the Chinese. The name derives from the Japanese words 'ori' meaning fold and 'kami' meaning paper. (Kami becomes gami when linked).

Technically speaking, no cutting, gluing or decoration of the paper is allowed. Although rules can be broken, I try not to cut the fabric; glue is cheating and any decoration is optional.

Many of the folding techniques originating in this ancient art of Origami can be constructed in fabric. Although, material is not as stiff as paper and flexes, it has an advantage - any fold that lies on the diagonal will roll back in an arc shape; therefore a simple origami design can made into a more complex shape by manipulating the folded edges.

One of my students, Margot Abrahams, takes great delight in sending me small samples of new ideas. She always omits the instructions, leaving me to fathom them out for myself. This usually results in levels of dust in the house and ironing piling up by the foot as I have to work out the method and then discover a way to teach the concept.

This particular design can be made from one piece of material, or it can be made from four squares stitched together. In the further developments at the end of the chapter, you will see many exciting possibilities for extending the idea.

Origami Twist Cushion with a smaller Origami Twist in the centre: Jennie Rayment

Origami Twist

This technique can be made from one big square of material or four squares stitched together to form a larger square. Sewing four squares together has greater potential for creativity as you can combine colour and/or fabric patterns to produce a fascinating result. Striped material can be most effective.

Medium-weight and crisply finished fabrics are preferable as they crease well. Fine and light-weight cloths are more difficult to manoeuvre into position and may not hold the folds well.

Take one square

1. Cut one 12½″ (31cm) square. Fold the square in half R/S out forming a rectangle.

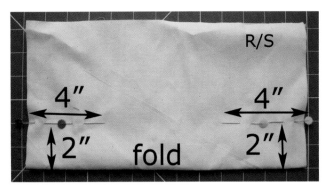

2. Place pins 2″ (5cm) from the fold, pinning through both layers of material. Put two pins in tandem (one behind the other) pinning a length of approximately 4″ (10cm) from either side. The pins must be parallel to the fold. These pinned sections form a tuck on either side of the square.

3. Fold one of the remaining two sides of the square in half R/S out. Place pins 2″ (5cm) from the fold as in the last stage. This forms a third pinned tuck.

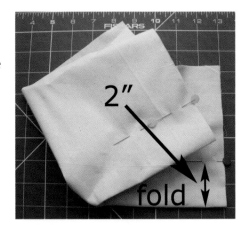

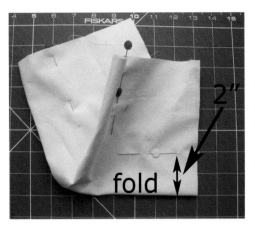

4. Repeat this pinning and folding with the last side of the square.

5. Open out the pinned shape and lay it on a flat surface (your knee is not a flat surface!). Four 2″ (5cm) tucks have been pinned in the centre of each side. Gently tweak the centre of the fabric upwards to form a sort of point - bit like a mountain.

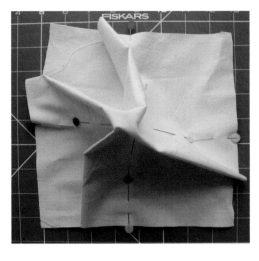

74

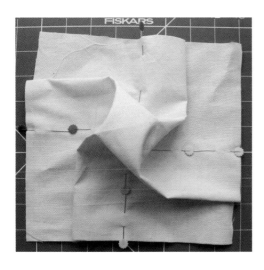 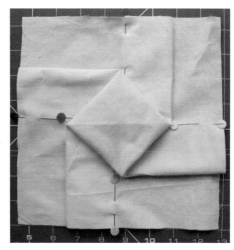

6. Slowly and gently rotate the four tucks round in the same direction. It doesn't matter if the tucks rotate clockwise or anti-clockwise.

With a careful pat and a prod the excess fabric in the centre will flatten to form a square. The four corners of this square will align exactly with the line of the pins. A little persuasion may be required.

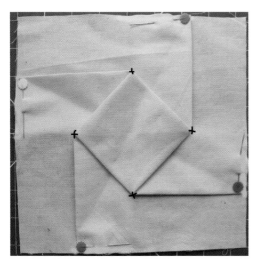

7. Press the work well. Pin the edges of the tucks to retain the shape.

8. Secure the centre square on all four corners with a small stitch through all layers

Having completed the folding, the work will measure about 8″ (20cm). It may need a little trimming to get it absolutely square.

Voilà an Origami Twist!

Take four squares

1. Cut four 5¾″ (14.5cm) squares from two contrasting colours and sew together as shown. Use ¼″ (0.75cm) S/A. Press the seams open and flat.

2. Fold the pressed square in half R/S out forming a rectangle and place pins at 1½″ (4cm) from the folds as explained in Stage 2 (page 74).

3. Follow the instructions in Stages 3 - 8 (page 74) and make an Origami Twist.

Amazingly the work will measure about 8" (20cm) square.

Whether you choose to cut one whole square or make a large square from four smaller squares, the same rule applies:

The pins can be placed at any distance from the fold up to half the total measurement of the folded side. Pins placed further from the fold produce a larger centre than pins placed nearer to the fold.

In the photograph, pins were placed 2" (5cm) from the fold as opposed to 1½" (4cm). Notice the difference in the size of the central square to the one in the photograph above.

Get ready to Play!

a. Roll all four edges of the central section inwards - they are all on the bias and will roll in a pleasing arc. Sew the arcs in place.

b. Lay a small square of contrasting material in the centre and roll the edges over the sides of this fabric. How about tucking a piece of wadding under before you stitch the rolled edges in place?

c. Why not make a smaller Origami Twist and insert in the centre (photograph page 73) or a square of pin tucked fabric?

d. Embellish the centre with embroidery, quilting or bead work.

d. Tuck Prairie Points or Somerset Patches under the centre square.

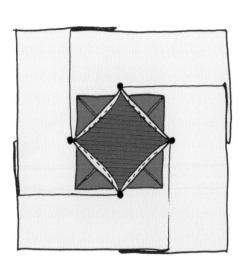

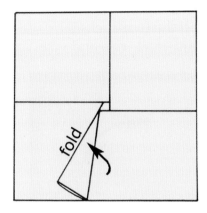

e. Look at the back of the work and play with the folds - this side could be used as the R/S if you preferred.

f. Instead of leaving the four tucks lying flat, lift them up and open to make a triangular shape. See what happens if you twist or roll the edges.

g. Make several small Origami Twists. Sew together for a novel cushion panel.

It pays to think about which way you rotate the folds of each Twist. Rotating all the folds in the same direction may be preferable although you could play!

Origami Twist with a Twist!

Try this for size.

1. Make the design to Stage 7 (page 75). Sew close to the raw edge to secure the tucks.

2. Lift up the centre square and turn it in the reverse direction to the four tucks. If the four tucks lie clockwise turn the centre anti-clockwise and vice versa.

Keep turning until the square cannot be rotated any more and all four tucks are pulling at an angle from the seam.

3. Secure the corners of the centre square in place. Sew through all the layers.

Play with the centre square and the tucks (described on pages 76 - 77).

Try the same idea with four squares stitched together.

Roll the edges of the central square over another fabric.

78

What about striped fabric?

Make a 12½″ (31cm) square for the centre of a cushion, bag or as a quilt block.

Following the technique outlined in Stages 1 - 8 (pages 74 - 75), cut an 18″ (45cm), square. Place the pins 2¾″ (6.5cm) from the fold.

Jiggle and wriggle a bit ..... with luck you will get a 12½″ (31cm) square. Ideal for a quilt block or centre of a cushion.

Make four of these in calico. Sew together, add a border, do a bit of quilting, bind the edge and... Hey Presto - a small cot quilt or wall-hanging.

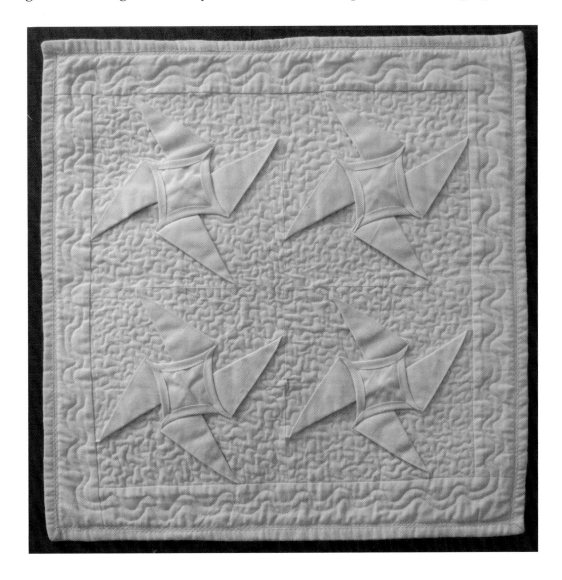

Extending the 'Bow Tie'

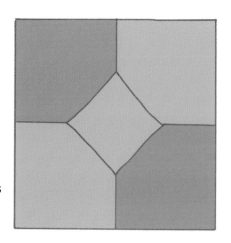

The 'Bow Tie' is the name of a traditional patchwork block which resembles a bow tie! There are several ways to construct this design.

The method described here takes five equal sized squares. One of the squares is inserted in the centre between the other four. Due to the construction technique, the sides of this inserted square have some pleasing textural possibilities - you can roll the edges, tuck folded shapes underneath and stuff the centre!

Once you understand the technique, the Bow Tie design can be incorporated in many places from garments to quilts, bags, cushions, tiebacks and more. Plus there is a nifty way to make the centre of the Bow Tie as a separate section and then it can be used as an appliqué for embellishment, to conceal a poorly pieced junction or cover a blemish.

Read on...

To create a green and purple 12½" (31cm) square, cut four 6½" (16.5cm) purple squares and one 6½" (16.5cm) green square.

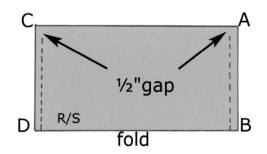

1. Fold the green square in half, R/S out forming a rectangle.

2. Stitch down either side using ¼" (0.75cm) S/A. **LEAVE a ½" (1.25cm) gap at the start of the seam.**

3. Sandwich one of the stitched sides of the rectangle between two of the purple squares. Place these squares R/S down. Align all the raw edges. Sew from the top to **X** leaving a ½" (1.25cm) gap at the start of the seam.

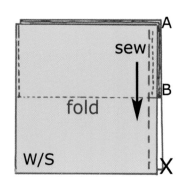

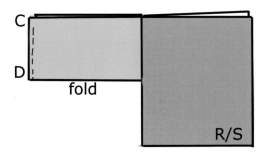
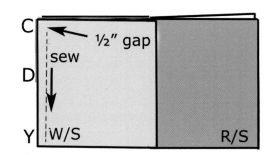

4. Fold both purple squares back to reveal the green rectangle. Lay the two remaining squares on the other end of the rectangle. Sew from the top to **Y** leaving a ½″ (1.25cm) gap at the start of the seam.

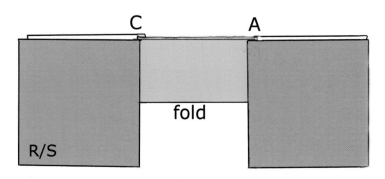

5. If you fold these squares back as well, you can see that the sides of the green rectangle are now enclosed in the two side seams. It could be described as resembling a bridge linking the two sets of squares - "A Bridge over Troubled Waters". Hopefully not!

6. Open the green folded rectangle (bridge) and bring **A** and **C** to touch (the green section forms a small pocket between the purple squares). Align the top edges of this pocket with the corresponding sides of the purple squares. Make sure that all the raw edges are level.

Sew from the centre to the end of the purple squares on either side. Leave ½″ (1.25cm) gap at the start of both seams. Press the seams open and flat as much as possible.

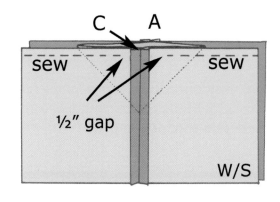

7. Turn over and… Bingo! The green square is neatly inserted between the four purple ones.

And that is the Bow Tie. A trifle boring at this stage... Keep reading.

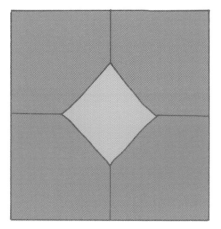

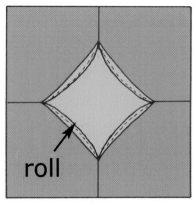

a. Roll the sides of the central green square inwards, stitch in place by hand or machine.

b. Cut another square in a contrasting colour. Place it on top of the green square. Roll the sides of the green square over the raw edges. Stitch the rolled sides in place.

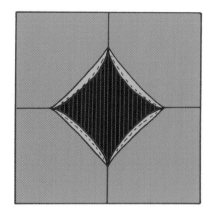

How about a square of pin tucked fabric (page 24) laid in the centre?

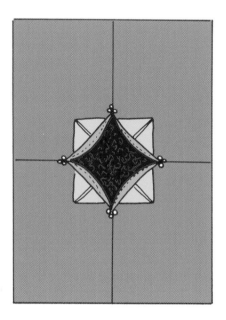

c. Consider tucking four Somerset Patches underneath the sides of the centre square before rolling the edges back and stitching in place?

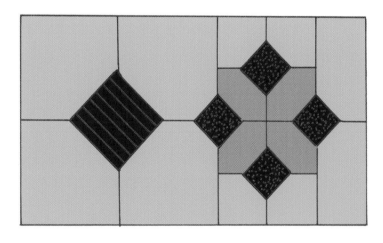

d. There is no reason why the inserted centre square has to be the same size as the others; it can be larger or smaller, and will still have the same properties.

So you can twist, roll, insert another material, decorate the central section and add Somerset Patches or indeed a Prairie Point or two.

The centre square need not be inserted between four squares; it can be set in any set of seams which meet at right angles. This is ideal for concealing a poorly pieced junction of four seams.

Bow Tie in a Circle

Panic not - this is a con! The circle is made from four squares. Puzzled... Read on.

The block described below makes a 5" (13cm) square when finished.

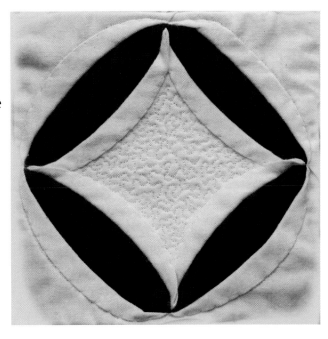

1. Cut four 3½" (8cm) squares in one colour and one 4½" (11cm) square for the centre.

2. Follow the instructions given in Stages 1 - 7 (pages 80 - 81) and make a Bow Tie.

Press the seams open and flat as shown on the left.

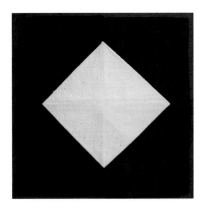

3. Cut four 9 cm (3½") squares in the same colour as the centre square unless you fancy a different colour.

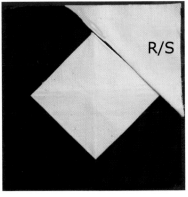

R/S

4. Press these squares diagonally in half forming triangles R/S out.

5. Lay one triangle on each corner. Place them in anti-clockwise order tucking the last one underneath the first.

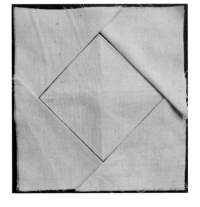

baste

6. Baste round the outer edge to hold all the triangles securely.

7. Sew across the junctions of the triangles with a small hand or machine stitch.

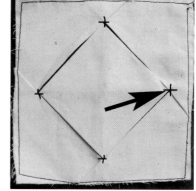

8. Roll back the edges of the centre section and the four triangles. Stitch in place.

There you go - a Bow Tie in a circle.

Try this design in different sizes and a variety of colours.

Combine five Bow Tie's and four Crossing Over the Tucks squares (page 28) to make an unusual Noughts and Crosses board.

A bit of fun!

Noughts & Crosses: Jennie Rayment

Appliqué a Bow Tie

This version of the Bow Tie can be made from any size of square and appliquéed in place. It is ideal for concealing a poorly pieced junction, covering a mistake or can be added as an intriguing textured element to a piece of work. It is a very useful trick to have at your finger tips.

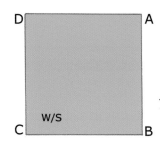

1. For a 6″ (15cm) finished square cut an 8½″ (22cm) square.

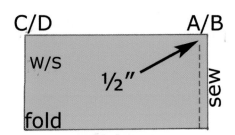

2. Fold the square in half forming a rectangle.

3. Sew down the **A/B** side using ¼″ (0.75cm) S/A. Leave a ½″ (1.25cm) gap at the start of the seam.

4. Fold **C** to touch **B**. Sew down this side leaving ½″ (1.25cm) gap at the start of the seam.

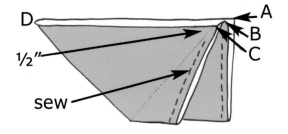

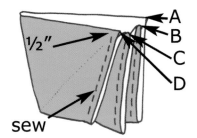

5. Fold **D** to touch **C** and as before, sew down the side leaving ½″ (1.25cm) gap at the start of the seam.

Almost getting boring!

6. Finally stitch the last two sides of the square together. Remember the gap!

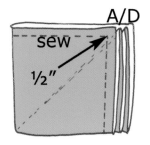

The theory behind this sewing method is to fold all four sides of the square and stitch along each side leaving... Wait for it... A ½″ (1.25cm) gap at the start of the seam. PTO

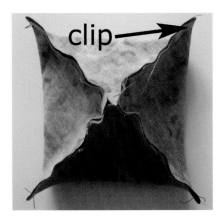

7. Having folded and stitched all the sides of the square the result should resemble the photograph. Do not worry about the hole at the centre of the seams - all will be well.

Carefully clip the corners off the end of each seam with sharp scissors. Do not cut through the seam.

8. Turn the square R/S out through the central hole.

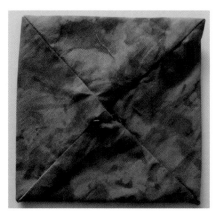

Gently poke all four corners out with a wooden barbeque skewer, a bamboo point turner or any other similar object. Don't ram the points of your scissors into the corner as you may pierce the fabric and make a hole. Press well.

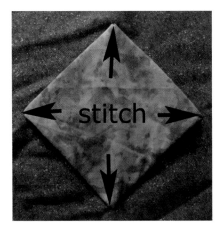
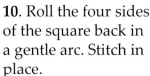

9. Arrange the square on another fabric, pin in place. Carefully stitch the four corners on to the other fabric.

10. Roll the four sides of the square back in a gentle arc. Stitch in place.

And... That is how you appliqué a Bow Tie!

Appliqué a Bow Tie on the shoulder yoke of a jacket or anywhere else you fancy.

Waistcoats & Jackets

Be individual: Construct your own tucked and textured garment using the techniques featured in this book.

The calico jacket in the photographs was made entirely from the 'Quilt-as-you-Go' method. It was created the day after returning to England on the 'red-eye' flight from Los Angeles. Despite suffering from the Beijing 'flu that had decimated L.A, I was determined not to give in to either jet-lag or any old virus. The sewing machine has always been a source of comfort in times of stress and "it seemed like a good idea at the time", but it did occur to me as I crouched over the fabric pieces feeling like death warmed up that staying in bed would have been preferable. Hence there are some interesting `designer' wobbles in the seams. Of course these little deviations enhance the unique individuality of the jacket!

Now you have read this book, you will be able to produce your own amazing masterpiece.

Calico Jacket with tucked panels and Bias Tucks on sleeve and on the front:
Jennie Rayment

Creating a Garment

1. Select a basic pattern.

Jacket and Waistcoat patterns need to be simple, with little tailoring and no darts. Loose fitting sleeves, possibly bat-wing, and bodices are essential; drop shoulders are also advantageous.

Trace the outline of the pattern on to light-weight sew-in interfacing; cut out, leaving

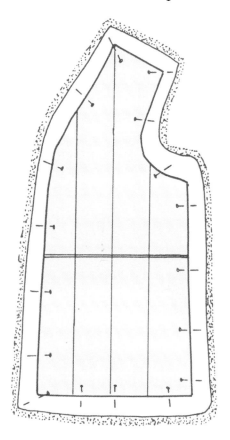

1" (2.5cm) or thereabouts excess interfacing around the outline. Drawing a few straight lines on the interfacing will help in positioning the textured pieces. Pin the interfacing on to 2oz wadding (batting) and cut round leaving a little extra wadding outside the edge of the interfacing. This forms the base for the textured samples. It pays to play safe - allow a little extra base materials. Adding the individual sections sometimes causes the base layers to contract.

The type of wadding (batting as it is referred to in other parts of the world) is your choice. I usually select a 2oz polyester wadding because it is light, washable, inexpensive and has a certain amount of 'loft'. (Loft is the term given to the springiness of any fibre and its ability to bounce back after being compressed.) I find that use of a light polyester wadding reduces the weight of the garments and prevents them getting too scrumpled. Some people prefer cotton, wool or even silk waddings. Check your choice of wadding will not shrink when washed otherwise that laboured over garment may become somewhat tight and that was not due to over ingestion of comestibles! (Amazing how doing the cross-word improves one's vocabulary, the answer to 9 down was 'comestible'.)

Choose a fine to medium-weight material to prevent the finished garment becoming too bulky due to the thickly layered textured sections. Silk, sateen, cotton and even a thin faux suede would be a good choice.

2. Make a variety of textured units; tucked panels and single Bias Tuck bands are possible selections. Pin the central design to the interfacing and wadding base, placing it parallel to the drawn lines. Baste the panel in place before adding any further sections. Attach the next pieces with the 'Quilt-as-you-Go' method (pages 37 - 40). It is preferable to intersperse heavily textured units with either plain strips or very lightly manipulated bands. Keep the sleeve and under-arm panels free from heavily pleated or tucked designs, otherwise you be unable to move easily and may not be able to bend your arms.

Continue building up the design with an assortment of textured strips. Allow extra material on all the outer lines of the pattern in case there has been some contraction in the overall fabric area whilst attaching the pieces.

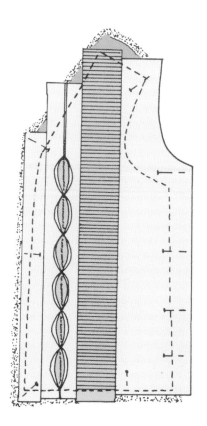

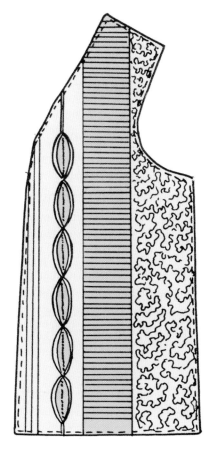

3. Once the various panels have been applied, secure all the layers by stitching round the outer edge.

Lay the paper pattern on this worked section, centring the pattern in the relevant places. Pin well. Cut out carefully. Stitch round the outside edge to secure.

4. Using the above technique - construct all the parts of the garment.

5. Trim as much wadding (batting) from the seams as possible to reduce bulk before making up the garment in accordance with the pattern instructions.

If the garment is being lined, for a professional appearance and to retain the lining, top stitch close to the edges of the garment.

Amaze everyone with your individual creation - it will be the only one in the World!

Calico Waistcoat with satin stitched embellished tucks and Bias Tucks down the centre: Jennie Rayment

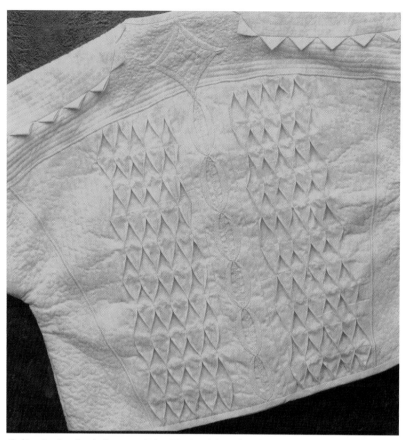

As an alternative to a loose lining, line the garment pieces individually.

Make up the pattern pieces to Stage 4 (page 79). Cut a piece of lining for all the sections and pin on the back (W/S together). Baste both layers carefully round the outside edges.

If you like to embellish, attach the darning/hopper or the walking/even-feed presser foot and sew through both layers. This will secure the layers firmly together and create an interesting stitched effect on the lining. (The use of either of these presser feet prevents the layers moving unevenly.)

Calico Jacket back features Bias Tuck with twisted tucks, Prairie Points with a Bow Tie applied to the shoulder area: Jennie Rayment.

On completion of any further stitching, sew the garment sections together and bind all raw edges.

Cotton Waistcoat constructed in 'Quilt-as-you-Go' technique with pin tucks, Bias Tuck and twisted tucks: Shelagh Jarvis

Finishing Techniques

This section covers bordering, quilting, piping, inserting zips into cushion backs, various frilling techniques and making a simple bag.

Having ploughed through all the examples, and created many samples, a splendid cushion will be absolutely essential on which to rest the weary head, and you will definitely need a bag to put everything in.

Adding a Border

Many of the samples will need to be bordered to enhance the appearance and neaten the edges; they can then be used for cushions or linked together to make quilts or wall-hangings.

Before you attempt to add borders to any piece of work, it is well worth trimming the edges and cutting them straight. Hopefully, it will not prove too difficult to convert the piece into a geometric shape of some description; a square is the most usual and easiest to adapt for a cushion, bag, box lid, or inclusion as a block in a quilt or wall-hanging. Sadly sometimes the four sides of a supposed square do not measure the same length. Don't worry. Pin accurately cut border strips to the sides and with a good push and pull, the completed piece should end up a perfect shape. (The technical term for this specific manoeuvre is 'easing'!)

To calculate the width of border required to increase the size of a square:

1. Measure across the work from raw edge to raw edge. Deduct the seam allowance you are using from this figure to produce the 'finished' size. (The finished size being the measurement of the work after all four sides have had a strip/border or binding attached.) Do not forget that there is a seam allowance on both edges so deduct twice the seam allowance.

2. Subtract this measurement from the desired 'finished' size of the square you wish to make. Divide the answer by two to produce the measurement of the width of the border. Remember to add your selected seam allowance to the answer.

Example: The work measures 11½" (29.5cm) so deduct the seam allowances 2 x ¼" (0.75cm) i.e. ½" (1.50cm) to equal the finished size 11" (28cm).

If the desired finished size of the work is 16" (40cm) then you must subtract 11" (28cm) from 16" (40cm). Divide the answer 5" (12cm) by 2 to give the measurement that has to be added to either side of the work i.e. 2½" (6cm).

NOW add on the seam allowances:- 2½" (6cm) + 2 x ¼"/0.75cm S/A = 3" (7.5cm).

This is the width of the strip you need to cut.

Having manoeuvred through these complicated mathematics and cut the border strip to the correct width, all you have to do is to cut it to the right length and stitch it on!

 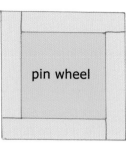 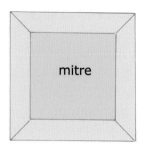

log cabin | pin wheel | mitre

Attaching a border

There are many ways to attach a border just like leaving your lover!

Personally I do not like the Log Cabin method of systematically attaching strips around the sides of the square. The seams are not symmetrical. The Pin Wheel and Mitre are good ways to attach a border although mitring the corners can be tricky.

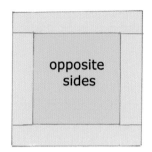 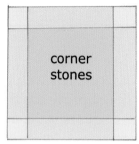

opposite sides | corner stones

Adding a border to the opposite sides is a simple and accurate method. Corner stones is equally easy and gives the option of using a different colour or textured design on the corner squares.

Always measure carefully as the work may well pull out of shape and distort if you just stitch a bit of fabric to the sides without cutting it to the correct length. Cutting the border strips to a set length and pinning to either end before stitching will keep the distortion under control. Some people like to lop - this is laying a length of fabric along the edge, sewing it on and lopping the ends off to fit the sides, this is not accurate... Please do not be a LOPER!

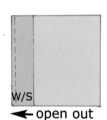 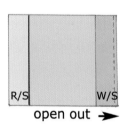 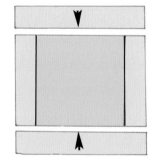 

W/S ← open out

R/S   open out → W/S

Opposite Sides

1. Measure the length of the sides first and cut two identical pieces this measurement. (The width will be whatever you choose.) Place one piece on either side, R/S down, pin well, stitch in place.

USE AN ACCURATE ¼ " (0.75cm) SEAM ALLOWANCE.

2. Open out. Measure the total length of the remaining sides and cut two more strips to this measurement. Pin as before, then stitch in place using the same S/A.

Frequently the stitching drifts inwards or outwards as you reach the end of the seam; keep concentrating on the stitching and try not to relax with relief until you have finished the seam.

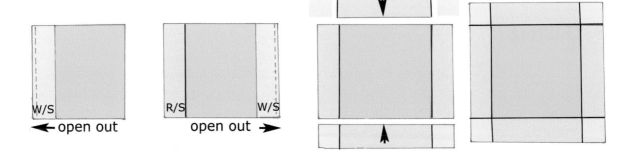

Corner Stones

1. Decide on the width of the border. Measure the sides of the block and cut four strips exactly this length x the selected width.

2. Cut four squares exactly the same size as the selected width of the border. (These are often referred to as corner stones hence the name for this bordering method.)

3. Stitch one strip to either side, R/S down. Open out.

4. Attach a square to both ends of the two remaining strips to make a longer strip.

5. Sew these elongated strips to the remaining sides. Match the seams at the junctions of the squares with the sides of the block.

For a novel idea, construct the corner stones from some form of textured design such as a Trumpet.

Cut the corner stone squares larger. Add on ½" (1.25cm) to the original measurement. Divide this larger square in half forming two triangles.

Fold another square into a Trumpet. Stitch the two triangles to form a square with the Trumpet inserted in the seam.

Keep playing with other textured ideas: Bias Tuck (page 47), Lifted Star (page 67) or an Origami Twist (page 74) would all be suitable.

Trumpet Bag with Somerset Patch inserts: Jennie Rayment

Quilting the Work

Hand Quilting

There is a wealth of information to be found on the Internet, a considerable amount is free to download, plus many books and articles on the subject are readily available from Quilting shops and Libraries for all those seeking to further their knowledge. So here is a brief synopsis.

The preparation for quilting involves placing the work on wadding (batting), preferably a light-weight one. A backing fabric is placed underneath the wadding and completes the 'sandwich' - top/wadding/backing. These three layers are tacked (basted in US) together with long hand stitches, safety pins (choose ones that don't rust) or purchase a tag gun. (Tag guns fire tiny plastic tags through the material thus holding the layers securely.)

Once the layers have been secured, stitch through all the materials with a running stitch. Relax about the size of the stitches. There is such a lot of "hype" talked about stitch length, quantity of stitches to the inch, etc. Why do all the stitches have to be very small? Must you sew 20 stitches to the inch? For instance, Sashiko, a Japanese style of quilting, displays large stitches with a thick gauge thread. Different hands work in different ways and everyone's flexibility varies; you may not be able to manipulate the needle in the same manner as that '20 stitches to the inch' friend of yours does. In addition, there is no doubt that fine, well-washed fabrics quilt more easily than un-washed firm weaves.

The rule you need to obey is...

Keep the stitch lengths and spaces between the stitches as even as possible.

"When executed correctly, hand-sewn quilt stitches are the same length on both the front and back of the quilt, and the spaces between them are all identical. Ideally, the smaller the stitch, the better; however, evenness and consistency of the stitches are more important than stitch size. And once this method becomes familiar, you will automatically sew smaller stitches." (Mary Stori)

Remember: Quilting is a way of defining a design, adding texture and anchoring the layers together. It should be a pleasing exercise to perform and not an arduous task.

Once all the quilting is complete, sew round the outer edges to anchor the three layers together before you finish the work with a binding or piping or incorporate it into another creation.

94   *Sashiko quilting stitch*

Machine Quilting

Once again, there is much information available in books, on videos/DVDs and the Internet. You can read or watch the right and wrong ways to machine quilt to your heart's content. Hence this short precis of the technique and possible pitfalls.

One problem occurs if you prepare the work as for hand quilting with a wadding and backing fabric then sew across the sandwich with the regular presser foot. Use of the regular presser foot will cause one of the layers to 'creep'. Reducing pressure on the presser foot can help (refer to your instruction book - some machines have this facility).

Use of a walking foot may solve the problem: This particular foot has its own set of feed dogs, which work in harmony with the feed dogs on the machine. In theory, the three layers (sandwich) of the quilt are pulled evenly; the top by the walking foot's feed dogs, the bottom by the machine's own, the wadding is fed through as the filling in the sandwich. Most makes of walking feet are very successful and are particularly good at long straight lines of stitch. The drawback to this natty gadget is its size, and manoeuvring a large quilt around under the foot is hard graft.

An alternative presser foot and the one I favour (as turning the quilt is much easier) is the darning foot, sometimes called a hopper, free-embroidery or a free-motion quilting foot. When this foot is attached to the machine and the presser foot lever is lowered, there is a small gap between the base of the darning foot and the throat plate. The feed dogs must be lowered or covered thus creating a greater space beneath the presser foot. As there is no pressure exerted by the presser foot and as the feed dogs are not active (can't feed/pull the work through) the quilt can be manoeuvred in any direction i.e. forwards, backwards and sideways. Indeed one is able to work 'freely', wandering at random in any direction in a defined or abstract pattern.

There is a wide selection of darning feet available these days in a variety of sizes. Some have an open-toe (cut away section in the front). It is worth seeking advice from your sewing machine store before you buy one.

BUT if you are only making a cushion, why bother to put a backing fabric on the work? Mount the work on 4oz wadding instead. Use of 4oz wadding underneath the cushion front prevents the wrinkles from the cushion pad or the filling either showing or coming through the cover.

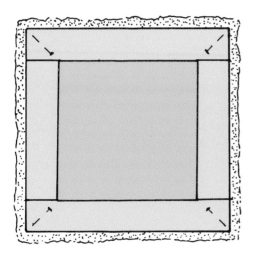

In addition, use of a thicker wadding will give the cushion a pleasingly plump appearance.

To prepare the cushion cover for machine quilting, cut a piece of 4oz wadding a little larger. Very gently press the work on to the wadding - do not over press as the wadding will melt. Pin the layers together on the corners, placing the pins pointing outwards.

As there are only two layers as opposed to three, the regular presser foot can be used. Two layers do not usually creep. Some people worry about sewing with wadding directly next to the feed dogs, the majority of machines will cope admirably. Should the feed dogs catch on the wadding whilst you are quilting, place a piece of paper or tissue paper underneath the work, this can be torn away afterwards.

There are several ways to machine quilt, choose which ever one you prefer. Here are three of them.

'Stitch in the Ditch'

This is quilting along the join (ditch) between two seams, the idea being to stay in the ditch and not deviate! No sewing on the fabric either side of the seam. To quilt a multi-coloured piece of work, match the thread to one of the colours and attempt to limit any meanders on to this fabric - stay in the ditch. (Use of invisible thread disguises any mistakes.)

Placing your hands gently either side of the seam and keeping it flat enables you to see the join more easily. Maintain a moderate even speed although some sewing machines cannot be operated this way; it's all or nothing. (This makes it very difficult to control!) Set a longer stitch length as the wadding causes the stitch to contract. When turning a corner, lower the needle into the seam, raise the presser foot and pivot round. Some presser feet are very hard to align as the size of the foot obscures the seam. In addition, I have discovered that wearing bi or vari-focals may make it difficult to see exactly where the seam line goes - a good excuse!

Top Stitching or Echo Quilting

Using the edge of the presser foot as a guide, follow round the outlines of the shape you wish to delineate. Again use a longer stitch length,. To turn a corner, lift the presser foot, drop the needle into the work and pivot round.

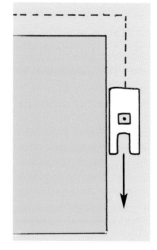

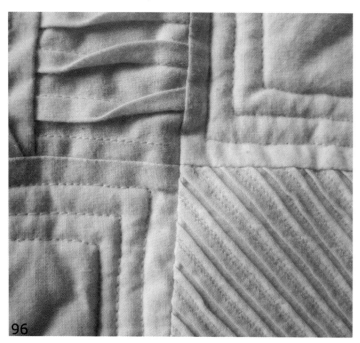

A contrasting choice of thread colour to the material can add interest to the finished appearance. But if you are not too confident, use matching threads to the fabric and the deviations from the chosen path will be less obvious.

Free Machine Quilting

There is no doubt that practice makes perfect; well, it improves it. This is one of those techniques that needs a relaxed operator (glass of wine is recommended before commencing - white wine for pale fabrics and red for dark ones in case it spills). Push the sewing machine further away than normal. Sit comfortably; lean towards the machine keeping the spine straight, pushing the bottom out and rest your elbows on the table to take the weight of your upper body. The wrists need to be free and flexible. Relax and drop your shoulders; students with rigid shoulders raised up to their ears do not perform so well.

So you are sitting correctly, have consumed the vino and relaxed. You have lowered the feed dogs, inserted the darning foot, positioned the work under the needle and all you have to do is construct a series of rounded squiggles. These should not cross over each other nor have points or spikes but flow evenly over the selected area .

Bet the telephone rings!

Try it; grasp the material firmly, do not have flat hands. Bring the lower thread to the top surface to prevent it tangling underneath. Maintain an even speed as you swing the work in a series of arcs (similar to steering a car). Relax.

Sometimes it not possible to obtain a darning foot for your machine but there may be a lever or knob that controls the amount of pressure on the presser foot (see instruction book). By reducing the pressure to zero and using the ordinary presser foot, it is possible to free machine quilt although not so easy.

Use of this technique will add more texture to the surface of the your work. It is difficult at first but keep experimenting and if you cannot achieve the random curves and even squiggles - have spikes!

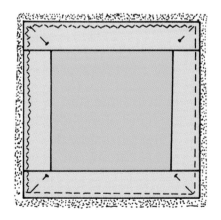

If you are making a cushion, once the work has been quilted, sew round the outside edge to secure all the layers; a long stitch length or wide zig-zag is ideal. It is not possible to add piping or any frill until the outer edge is stabilised

Decorative Edging Techniques

Piping

Piping the edge gives an pleasingly tactile edge to the finished objet d'art and is not difficult on the machine if you use this method. (If you are working by hand follow the same instructions.) As ever, there are a variety of methods of construction, and the technique suggested may be contrary to other well-established ways.

In this technique, for all cotton, chintz and calico type materials **cut the strips to cover the cord across the material from selvedge to selvedge** (side to side); there is no necessity to cut on the bias unless you are working with thickly woven materials such as brocades, velvet or any striped material, then a bias-cut strip is better.

Should you wish to cut strips on the bias use the rotary cutter and join the strips, the tube method of producing a long bias strip is complicated, it is rarely as straight as strips cut with the rotary cutter and some of the seams are very close together.

How to Pipe

1. Measure the length or circumference of the piece. Cut sufficient 1½" (4cm) wide strips to fit this measurement, if necessary join the strips together with a straight seam, trim any excess and open the seam out, and press flat.

2. Cut the same measurement of 4mm (medium sized) piping cord. (Beware: Some of the inexpensive cords shrink considerably, wash the cord in hot water to prevent further shrinkage on future laundering of the finished article. If you follow this method the better quality cords need not be washed. Who wants to waste time washing cord?)

3. Put the zipper foot on the machine setting the needle on your left, i.e. away from the body of the machine. (Bernina users, remember to move the needle position to the far side.)

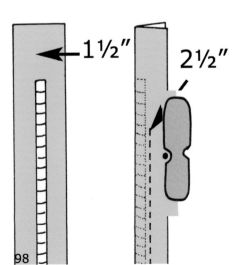

Set a long stitch length for speed. Lay the cord on the wrong side of the strip, setting down by 1½" (4cm). Fold the fabric over, lining up the edges.

4. Commence sewing 1" (2.5cm) below the start of the cord. Place the finger of your left hand alongside the cord and hold both the edges of the fabric together with the right hand; there is no necessity to pin. Sew to the end.

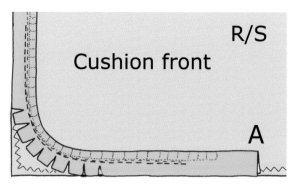

Cushion front

R/S

A

5. Place the piping on the R/S in the centre of lower side of the cushion front or in the middle of any side if there is no distinction. Lay the open end down first.

6. Sew clockwise round the work, matching the edges of the piping to the edges of the sample.

Stop approximately 3″ (7.5cm) from a corner, clip well and curve the cord in a gentle arc. Too sharp a curve will result in a pointed corner to the finished article. Do not pin the piping as a better result will be obtained by letting the piping flex round by itself; if you pin the piping in place then it may stretch whilst being pinned and not lie flat

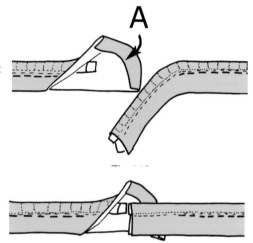

A

7. To join the cord, continue round the shape until you approach the start of the cord; stop 3″ (7.5cm) away.

At **A** fold the raw edge ¼″ (0.75cm) over to the W/S.

Trim the other end of the piping, butting it up exactly to the start of the cord. Butt both ends together.

Fold the excess fabric over this join and sew past.

As the ends of the cord are butted together and hidden in two layers of fabric, this junction will conceal any shrinkage in the cord when washed. (You can tell if your friends have washed their cushions by gently feeling this junction and seeing if there is a gap!)

Ruched Piping

For an enhanced textural effect make ruched piping instead. It requires a wider strip than the previous method.

1. Measure the length of ruched piping required, multiply this measurement by three. Cut sufficient 2" (5cm) strips and join if needed to make the correct length. Join the strips with a narrow S/A and press the seam open.

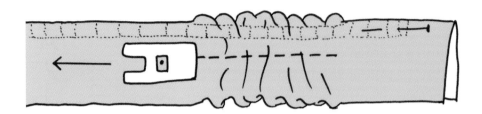

2. Cut a piece of cord the exact length of the work. Pin the end of the cord firmly to the start of the strip, setting the cord 1½" (4cm) from the start of the strip. Place the normal straight stitch presser foot on the machine. Fold the fabric over, matching the edges, and sew, keeping edge of the presser foot running alongside the piping cord. The cord is enclosed in a stitched channel.

When you reach the end of the cord, pull the cord up through the stitched channel; the fabric will ruche along the cord.

3. Continue sewing and ruching until the end of the fabric strip and cord, then pin the cord to the strip to prevent it un-gathering. Spread the gathers evenly along the cord.

This is applied in the same manner as the previous method (pages 98 - 99), although there is no need to clip the corner curves. It is difficult to complete the final butting of the cords and requires a little persuasion; but the finished effect is delightful.

Watch that the cord does not become too tight round the corners - ease gently.

Frilling Techniques

Frills can be gathered, pleated, ruched or contain piping. The frill may be as full as you like, but it will appear more luxurious if there is plenty of material.

There's nothing like a good frill to enhance your work!

Gathered Frills

Measure the length of frill required and multiply this figure by either two or three (three times the length will be a more ornate frill). Decide on the depth of frill required, then cut strips of fabric twice this measurement, add a ½" (1.25cm) S/A to either side. Also remember to cut the strips across the fabric - selvedge to selvedge.

1. Join all the lengths together to form a long strip, trimming seams and pressing open. Join the ends of the strip together to make a circle. Check there is no twist in the circle.

2. Fold in half, press well. Stitch along the lower edge to prevent movement when gathering.

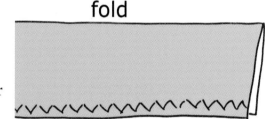

3. Gathering can be done in a variety of ways. Before starting, mark the length of the frill in four equal stages - use a pin or light pencil mark.

a. By hand - gather up the four sections to fit the desired space.

b. Use a long stitch on the sewing machine - gather the four sections individually (there is less chance of the thread snapping).

c. Use a Ruffler - this is a special gadget that is attached to the machine and will ruffle the fabric. It is an optional extra for the machine although some older models may have one lurking in the attachments box; it resembles an instrument of Mediaeval torture! I admit it ruffles beautifully, but the ultimate measurement of the frill is pure guesswork, as the printed instructions are unfathomable, and omit to take account of the thickness of the fabric, size of stitch length etc. So it is by guess and by God, but it pulls out easily and you can always do it again.

The ruffler is not the same as the gathering foot that some machines have in their accessory box. The gathering foot will gather fine fabrics and lace but not always anything thick.

d. Use the cord method - this is ideal for any machine.

Cut a length of cord, the circumference of the work plus 2" - 3" (5cm - 7.5cm). Use button hole thread, fine strong crotchet thread, stranded embroidery silk or similar.

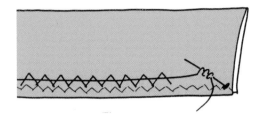

Pin the start of the cord onto the edge of the frill and set the machine for a wide zig-zag, the widest and longest it will do. Sew over the cord; by pulling it up above the foot and through the slit, you are less likely to stitch through the cord.

When you reach the end of the cord, raise the presser foot and pull more cord through. This will start to gather up the material as it goes. This is the same situation as pushing the wire through the heading of a net curtain; the wire is the correct length and the curtain will ruche on to the wire.

Pin the end of the cord to the end of the strip; as the cord was the correct length, the frill will fit the work.

4. Pin the frill to the work, lining all the edges. Stitch, using the zipper foot, ensuring that plenty of frill is arranged on the corners, or it will appear tight.

Do not panic if the frill does not go hard up to the piping; all the extra stitching now showing will be concealed when the back is applied.

It is not always necessary to pipe but you may find it easier when adding a frill, as the ridge of the piping provides a guideline to sew round

Ruched Frill

See Ruched Frill (page 30).

Measure the circumference or the length of the article to be frilled. Make the frill the same dimensions as described in the Frill section.

Remember to divide the fabric into four equal parts, then gather either side of the strip, independently. Adjust the quantity of frill so it will fit the sides. Fold over and sew the edges together before applying as described above.

Bow Tie cushion with ruched frill: Jennie Rayment

Cutting the strips on the bias produces a slightly more rounded appearance to the frill edge; straight cut strips create a crisper, more ridged effect.

Piped Frill

This was discovered by accident. I am not sure whether it is a set formula or not. The piping cord is enclosed in this frill and the frill drawn up on it. This is a combination of ruched piping and a frill; it saves fabric, a bit of time, and it is different.

1. Decide on the overall depth of the frill (page 101) and allow 1" (2.5cm) S/A on both edges. Measure the length of frill required and multiply this figure by two. Cut the sufficient strips to make this length (use the rotary cutter) and join together, trimming and pressing the seams open. Fold the strip in half and press.

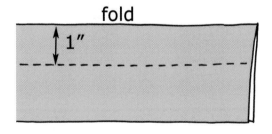

2. Cut the cord the exact length of the work. Attach the normal straight stitch foot to the machine and sew along the frill 1" (2.5cm) from the edge. Open the fabric out, and lay in the cord inside. Pin the end of the cord to the fabric.

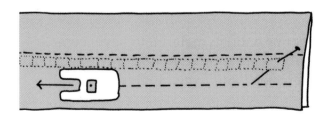

3. Leaving the normal presser foot in place, sew along the cord as described in Ruched Piping, gathering up the material. When you reach the end of the cord. pin it to the end of the fabric.

103

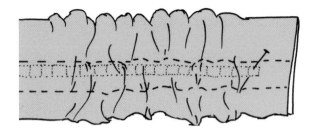

4. Shuffle the gathers evenly along the cord. It is now ready to apply. (See pages 98 - 99.)

Be careful when you butt the ends of the cord together - it is a bit of a jiggle!
A modicum of patience might be required.

Inserting a Zip

Although I am an ardent sewing machine fan, inserting a zip can also be done by hand using a series of small back stitches where any machine sewing is indicated.

When purchasing a zip, it is not important for the zip to measure the full width of the article; 16"- 18" (40cm - 45cm) pads can be fitted through the aperture of a 12" (30cm) zip. Alternatively, extra long plastic toothed zips bought in the bargain store are ideal as they be trimmed easily to the required length.

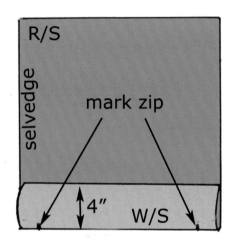

1. Measure the overall width and length of the article. Cut a rectangle of fabric the same width but 1½" (4cm) longer. Cut out with the longer length down the grain, i.e. selvedge down the length.

2. Fold up 4" (10cm) on the longer sides, R/S together. Press the fold. Lay the zip on the fold and with a pencil, mark the beginning and end of the teeth, or approximately 1½" (4cm) from outer edge.

3. Sew from the outer edge to this mark using ¾" (2cm) S/A. Sew forward then reverse for a firm seam.

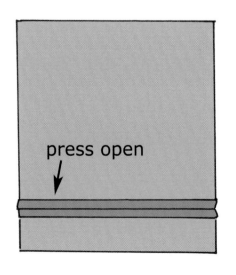

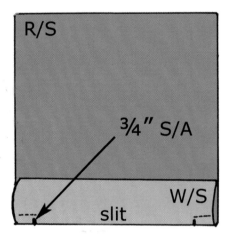

4. Slit this edge and press open the seams.

Should there not be enough material to have a whole piece for the back, there is no reason why two sections cannot be used instead and joined with a ¾" (2cm) seam.

5. Lay the zip in the opening, with the head positioned as shown in the diagram.

Remember to have the zip placed face down, otherwise it is very hard to open!

Fasten the zip head end to the seam with a pin on either side.

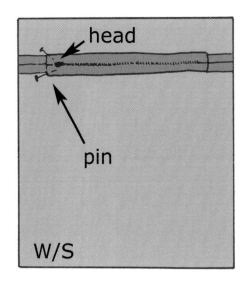

6. Put the zipper foot on the machine; the foot is now on the left of the needle, i.e. needle on the inside. Turn the material over, R/S facing. Open the zip 2" (5cm) and commence sewing with a small seam, approximately ¼" (0.75cm).

Drop the needle into the work when the zip head is reached, raise the presser foot, slide the zip head past. Continue sewing until the end of the zip, lining up the fold with mid-point of the zip teeth, turn and sew across the end. Watch the needle if the zip teeth are metal!

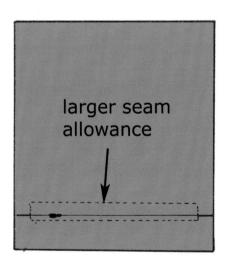

7. Take a slightly larger seam on the return journey, lapping the top fold fractionally over the lower fold. This overlap will prevent the zip teeth showing when the pad is inserted.

Drop the needle into the work approximately 2" (5cm) from end, slide the zip head past and continue to the end; turn and complete the seam. Finish off by pulling threads through to the back, tie together and either trim or weave ends into fabric seam with a needle.

Congratulate yourself! Open the zip a few inches or it will be awkward to move when you have applied the back.

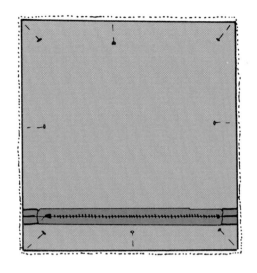

Applying the zipped back to the cushion

1. Pin the back to the cushion front R/S together, positioning the zip at the bottom.

Attach the zipper foot to the sewing machine. Move the needle to the left side of the presser foot. Place the edge of the foot as close as you can to the edge of the piping cord.

Do not stitch inside the cord or it will disappear when you turn the work right side out!

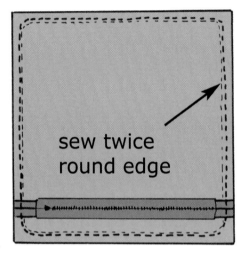

sew twice
round edge

Push really hard with the left hand fingertips, trying to get the needle close to the cord. The arm may well ache with the strain. Sew round twice, setting the needle and foot outside the cord.

Bernina users cannot do this as the needle fits inside the presser foot. You can push until you are blue in the face and it will not succeed. Purchase a Piping Foot to solve this problem; the groove on the underside of this presser foot will sit on the cord allowing the needle to travel next to the piping.

2. Turn to the right side and check that all the previous lines of stitching are now hidden; if not, sew again and push a little harder especially on the corners. TRY not to stitch over the cord or it will vanish!

Clip and trim any excess material. Push a pad in and

ADMIRE!

Buying a Pad

Many different types of cushion pads are available, ranging from feather to man-made fibres such as polyester. Select which is the most suitable for your requirements.

Pads should always be 1″ (2.5cm) larger than the finished item, or the same size as the incomplete article before you pipe it.

Making a Simple Bag

This is the fastest and quickest lined bag with handles that I have ever made. It is so easy, and the principle can be adapted for constructing any size of bag.

"Oh yes", we have all heard that before, but I promise you all that this is the first bag from Lesson 1 in my beginner's class, and there have been many made over the years of classes. I can spot any of these students a mile away as they still use the bag!

It requires four pieces of material exactly the same size; two outside ones which could be textured samples plus two pieces of lining material - calico is admirable. Quilt the outside sections on to 4oz wadding (not forgetting to sew round the outer edges to secure the top layer to the wadding). In addition, make two handles (page 36). Remember to turn the raw edge under when you construct the handles; do ensure they are both the same length. They can be any length you like, 14" (35cm) is a reasonable length for short handles, increase the length if desired.

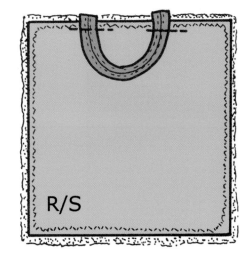

1. Lay one handle on the top edge of one outside section. Space the ends of the handle at one-third intervals approximately. Stitch the handle ends firmly, sew back and forward within the seam allowance.

Repeat this operation with the other handle and outside section.

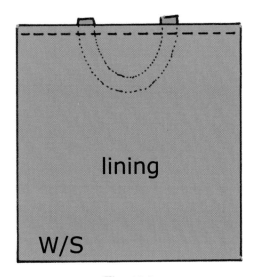

2. Lay the lining on top, R/S together. Attach the lining by sewing along the top edge over the handle ends. Use a generous ¼" (0.75cm) S/A.

Repeat this stage with the other outside section and the remaining piece of lining.

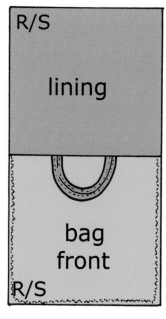

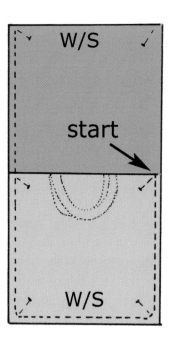

3. Open out both of the pieces to form two rectangles. Lay the two rectangles R/S together. Pin the layers matching the centre seam.

Commence sewing from the centre seam. This ensures the seam between the lining and the outside sections matches.

Sew a gentle arc round the corners of the outside sections. Stitch to the end of the lining.

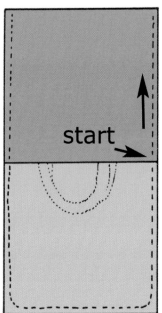

4. Flip the work over and complete the last seam. Trim any excess wadding and material.

5. Turn the bag to the right side through the gap. Close the gap with a few stitches. Push the lining into the bag and poke the corners out. Finally, to retain the lining within the bag, top stitch round the edge, taking care over the thick side seams.

Well, was I right ?

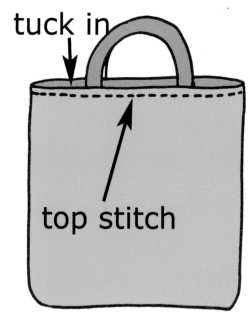

tuck in

top stitch

Crazy Patchwork Bag with fancy handles:
Chris Frampton

Now you have learnt so many different ways to tuck and twiddle, weave, ruche and scrunch, bedazzle with the bias, tweak a trumpet, lift a star, get knitted and knotted and oh sew much more; why not combine all these fabulous ideas and make a quilt?

It's easy, it's fun and it's different, and making mistakes will not matter!

Calico Quilt 84" x 64" featuring Trumpets, Bias Tucks, weaving, ruching, tucks and more:
Shelagh Jarvis

Glossary

Backing: The fabric used underneath a sample or the underside of a cushion or quilt.

Baste: Securing of layers with a long stitch to prevent movement.

Batting: Wadding or filling frequently made from polyester fibres used between or underneath fabric for quilting purposes.

Bias: Diagonal of the woven grain (45° to the selvedge).

Borders: Fabric attached to the outer edges to frame the sample.

Box Pleats: Pairs of pleats folded towards each other.

Calico: Plain woven strong cotton cloth sometimes bleached with a distinctive fleck in the weave. (British definition). Printed floral cotton fabric. (US definition).

Cathedral Window Patchwork: Traditional design constructed from folded and stitched squares.

Chintz: Close-weave shiny cotton cloth with a resin coating that gives it the characteristic sheen.

Cretonne: A washable hard-wearing fabric similar to unglazed chintz; liable to shrink.

Crimplene: Stretchy material produced from man-made fibres.

Gaberdine: A lightweight closely woven fabric with a prominent diagonal rib.

Grain: Direction of the weave. Weft fibres run across from selvedge to selvedge. Warp fibres are parallel to the selvedge.

Log Cabin/Pineapple Patchwork: Traditional designs made from strips of material.

Mercerised Cotton: Treated to look like silk.

Muslin: Fine soft cotton fabric resembling gauze in appearance (British definition).

Pin Tucks: Fine tucks sometimes enclosing a cord.

Ruche/Ruching: Gathered material often in a strip, used for decorative effect.

Satin Stitch: The zig-zag effect produced by increasing the stitch width and decreasing the stitch length on the sewing machine.

Seam Allowance or S/A: Distance between the stitch line and the edge of the fabric.

Selvedge/selvage: the firm edges of the fabric running parallel to the warp threads.

Somerset/Folded Patchwork: Design made with folded squares of fabric, worked from the centre outwards on lines relating to equal points of the compass

Space Dyed Threads: Fibres dyed in a variety of separate colours.

Suffolk Puff: Gathered circle of fabric sometimes stuffed with wadding or containing an inserted circle of contrasting material. Widely used in Victorian times.

Vanishing Pen: Pen containing special chemical ink that disappears in time.

Vilene: Interfacing developed from bonded fibres

Wadding: Batting or filling frequently made from polyester fibres used between or underneath fabric for quilting purposes.

Warp: Threads stretched lengthwise on the loom.

Weft: Threads woven into and crossing the warp.

Bibliography

Conran, Terence. The Soft Furnishings Book. Book Club Associates, 1986

Fishburn, Angela. Curtains and Window Treatments.   B.T. Batsford Ltd, 1982.

Frutiger, Adrian. Signs and Symbols. Studio Editions 1991.

Halsey, Mike & Youngmark, Lore. Foundations of Weaving. David & Charles, 1986.

Jackson, Paul. Encylopedia of Origami & Papercraft Techniques. Headline Books 1991.

Poster, Donna. The Quilter's Guide to Rotary Cutting. Chiltern Book Company, 1991

Play on!

TUCKS & TEXTURES TWO
Fiddle with Fabric - Dip into Dye

A totally different and separate book from 'Tucks Textures & Pleats'. It explores the versatility of Cathedral Windows, the diversity of Log Cabin Corners, a bit of Vandalism and Interlocking Shapes, reveals the secret of Sculptured Spheres, unveils the magic of Microwave Dyeing plus projects on the Pilgrim Scrip and other intriguing bags, Textured Landscapes, and even the Calico Hat.

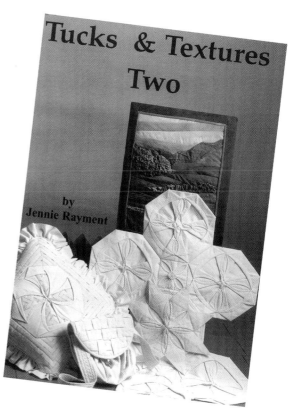

(112 A4 pages: 200+ diagrams and colour plates: perfect bound.)

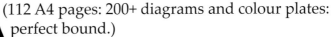

FOLDY ROLLY PATCHWORK PZZAZZ
Tactile twiddling for all

Twelve blocks and related projects to entrance, educate and entertain. From textured quilt blocks to bags, quags, cushions and table mats, these ingeniously simple yet fabulously folded novel techniques are ideal for all stitchers of every ability. Full of colour with every stage presented in clear photographic format. Helpful hints and useful tips abound plus lighthearted tales of travel and derring-do! (112 A4 pages: 400+ photographs & diagrams, perfect bound)

J. R. Publications
5 Queen Street, Emsworth,
Hampshire PO10 7BJ England
Phone/Fax: +44 (0) 1243 374860
e-mail: jenrayment@aol.com www.jennierayment.com

Jennie Rayment

This skinnyish, reddish-haired, slightly wacky Brit is totally obsessed with 'Nipping and Tucking' - fabric manipulation and surface texture. Unique in her field, she's now internationally known for her quick, simple, innovative and original techniques with manipulated material and her hilarious lectures with real 'Strip, Show and Tell'.

Jennie teaches a wide variety of classes for all levels and abilities of sewers from patchworkers, quilters and embroiderers to fashion, soft furnishing and home décor enthusiasts. Indeed, anyone interested in any form of needlework will be totally captivated by her deviously ingenious textural designs and can benefit from the wealth of creative ideas arising from her magic manipulations.

Although, much of her work is created in simple calico known as muslin in the USA, her elegant ideas and natty notions may be adapted for any type of fabric and used to make quilts, wall-hangings, boxes, baskets, cushions, table linen and of course fashion garments and accessories. She works and teaches on a variety of sewing machines from Bernina, Husqvarna, Pfaff to Brother, Janome and Elna but her delectable creations can be made by hand.

With seven books on fabric manipulation techniques, many articles and a variety of patterns, Jennie's material magic goes on and on.

Jennie Rayment
5 Queen Street, Emsworth,
Hampshire PO10 7BJ England
Phone/Fax: +44 (0) 1243 374860
e-mail: jenrayment@aol.com

www.jennierayment.com